REDISCOVERING

THE PASTORAL CALL
AND RESPONSIBILITIES

BY

REVEREND DR. JEFFERY A. GLADNEY

ISBN-978-1-960853-47-9

Liberation's Publishing LLC
Columbus - Mississippi

Presented by: Rev. Dr. Jeffery A. Gladney
Pastor, Author, and Community Leader
Tupelo, Mississippi, 38804
662-844-8713   662-255-1731
e-mail: jvglad@comcast.net

REDISCOVERING

THE PASTORAL CALL AND RESPONSIBILITIES

Table of Content

"These set of sermons and this book are gifts from God and the work of the Holy Spirit. I thank God for my father, who is now in heaven, smiling down on me from above. I thank God for Dr. Henry A. Gladney, who inspired me to do God's will at all costs. I also would like to thank my mother, Magnolia Gladney, my wife, Valeria T. M. Gladney, and my son, Joshua Gladney. Much is owed to Red Oak Grove Missionary Baptist Church in Tupelo, Mississippi, where I served as God's spokesperson.

A special thanks goes out to Rev. Samuel C. Tolbert, Jr., President; Dr. Joel D. Taylor, Congress Director; Rev. A. W. Anthony Mays, Congress Dean, National Baptist Congress of Christian Education and Discipleship. I owe an awesome debt of gratitude to George and Katie Moore for their support and love. I pray that these messages will inspire and bless you as you do God's will."

-Reverend Dr. Jeffery Gladney
In His Service

INTRODUCTION

"I found this excerpt interesting, and I would like to start this session off with this inspirational reading. This is an encouragement to those who are limping in leadership. I entered ministry after a long career in the business world. I had significant life and leadership experience, but honestly, some of it was learned through tremendously painful experiences. Not only did I lack the pedigree of most pastors, but I also found myself entering ministry following a sizable business loss – where we were forced to sell our business and basically start over financially – when God called me into ministry."

I Entered Ministry Limping

"The truth is the best leaders I know have a limp of some nature. It may not be visible, but if you are around them long enough, they will display remnants of a previous injury. They may have experienced a failure that crippled them for a season. They may have messed up, made a mistake, or lost their way. They may have been injured by others. And, as a result, they may have even been tempted to quit, but they pushed forward, never to be the same again.

If this is your story – if you have a limp and you're in leadership – I have a few suggestions." Here are 5 ways to lead well when you have a limp.

Don't Hide Your Limp

There is most likely a younger leader around you who feels they've lost their way – or will someday. They need your guidance. They need your encouragement. They need to see by example they can get up again and move forward. You don't have to wear a sign around your neck or tell everyone you meet about your limp, but you shouldn't pretend it isn't true, either. Your story is your story.

Your limp may be God's way of keeping you humble. Rahab of the Bible never lost her title as a harlot, even in the faith chapter (Hebrews 11). It reminds me that the past is my past – I can't change it or hide it, for long. A great leader never forgets where they came from.

Don't Be a Martyr

No one enjoys a complainer or someone who is always making excuses. You suffered a failure. You had a setback. You made a critical error. You sinned. Others sinned against you. Don't wallow in your misery forever. It's not an attractive characteristic in leadership. One of my favorite verses for those of us who limp is Ecclesiastes 11:3. Look it up – recognize it's true – and deal with it. It's what you do after the fall that matters most.

Allow It to Strengthen You!

You have two choices with a limp. You can allow your limp to make you a better person and leader. Or, you can let it keep you from ever being whole again – and never realize your full potential.

Grace is available if you will receive it. There may be forgiveness you need to seek or extend. You may need to do other "right things". But, let your limp strengthen your leadership abilities, even if it's simply learning what not to do next time. Most of us learn more in the hard times than the easy times. Most likely, you will also.

Be Empathetic.

There is nothing worse than one with a limp refusing to recognize others who limp. Always remember others have struggles too. If not now, they will. They're finding their way, just as you did. Extend grace as grace has been given to you.

Keep Limping Across the Finish Line.

Don't give up. Great leaders proudly limp to victory. They cheer on others who limp. They steadfastly keep going towards the goal. And, in the process, they encourage a lot of people and accomplish great things.

Limp well my friend, limp well!

THE **?** BIG QUESTION? **Are you leading with a limp? How has it shaped your leadership?**

_____
_____
_____
_____
_____

Sorry to say, at the outset of this class that in many churches it seems that the pastor just cannot do anything right. No matter how sincere he may be or how hard he tries, there is always someone that stands ready to find fault and criticize.

It has been described in this way:

- If the pastor is young, he lacks experience; if his hair is gray, he's too old for the young people.

- If he has five or six children, he has too many; if he has none, he's setting a bad example.

- If he preaches from notes, he has canned sermons and is dry; if his messages are extemporaneous, he isn't deep enough.

- If he caters to the poor in the church, he's playing to the grandstand; if he pays attention to the wealthy, he's trying to be an aristocrat.

- If he uses too many illustrations, he's neglecting the Bible, if he does not include stories, he isn't clear.

- If he drives an old car, he shames his congregation; if he buys a new one, he's setting his affection on earthly things.

- If he preaches all the time, the congregation gets tired of hearing just one man; if he invites guest ministers, he's shirking his responsibility.

Now I realize that the previous situation may be exaggerated, but they do emphasize general attitudes in many places. It doesn't seem to make much difference where you go or which church you attend, there's always that one group/faction that is "down" on the pastor.[1]

With hardly an exception they don't want pastors at all. They mangers of their religious company. They want a pastor they can follow so they won't have to bother with following Jesus anymore.[2]

Some time ago I read an article titled "Qualifications of a Good Pastor," and it further underscored the unreasonable demands often placed on God's servants it reads as follows:

A Good Pastor must have:

The strength of an ox

The tenacity of a bulldog

The daring of a lion

The wisdom of an owl

The harmlessness of a sheep

The industry of a beaver

The gentleness of a sheep

The versatility of a chameleon

---

[1] Walker H. John, A Fresh Look at the New Testament Deacon, Orman Press. pp71-72

[2] Peterson Eugene, Darwin Marva, The Unnecessary Pastor Rediscovering the Call, Regent College Publishing, pp4

The vision of an eagle

The hide of a rhinoceros

The perspective of a giraffe

The endurance of a camel

The bounce of a kangaroo

The stomach of a horse

The disposition of an angel

The loyalty of an apostle

The faithfulness of a prophet

The tenderness of a shepherd

And still he could not please everybody

The title of the book is re-discovering the pastoral call and responsibility suggests within itself that the call at one point was clear and the responsibility was understood. The Bible plainly says in Psalms 85:6 Wilt thou not revive us again: that thy people may rejoice in thee? (KJV)

Again, suggests that the people once were revived. We are going to seek to find the joy that we once had, if we don't have it anymore, or take the joy we have to a new level. Allow me to say at the outset of this class that we are called to do what Timothy commands us to do in: 2 Timothy 4:2 which says, "Preach the word; be instant in season, out of season; reprove, rebuke, exhort with all longsuffering and doctrine."

Being in season is when they want to hear you. It's easy to preach when you are in season, but seasons change. You also have to be instant out of season as well. Therein lies the juxtapose position we have been placed in. We have been called to preach when they don't want to hear us and when they do.

The wrestling question is how do you handle your out of season time?

The Bible says we handle our out of season time by what? 1 Thessalonians 5:17 encourages us to do which is "Pray without ceasing." That is one way to rediscover the call is to spend time with God in prayer. "Little Prayer, Little Power, Much Prayer Much Power."

No matter what you are going through never be accused of not preaching. Let people say what they want to say about you, but never let it be said you lost the ability to make the certain sound of the trumpet.

1 Corinthians 14:7-9 says Even things without life, whether flute or harp, when they make a sound, unless they make a distinction in the sounds, how will it be known what is piped or played? For if the trumpet makes an uncertain sound, who will prepare for battle? So likewise you, unless you utter by the tongue words easy to understand, how will it be known what is spoken?

That is what Dr. Samuel D. Proctor talked about in his book he Certain Sound of the Trumpet. Paul also gives us the Biblical foundation for the purpose of preaching 1 Corinthians 14:3 says But he who prophesies speaks edification and exhortation and comfort to men. This is because one that prophesies speaks in the language of his audience. A prophet is one speaks the Word of God for edification of believers.

Second, prophecy is for exhortation, or encouragement, because living in this sinful world is discouraging. Third, prophecy is for comfort such as at funerals, etc.

All I'm trying to say is don't lose the ability to use your instrument.

PART ONE

A man found an eagle's egg and put it in a nest of a barnyard hen. The eaglet hatched and the brood of chicks grew up. All his life the eagle did what the barnyard chicks did, thinking he was a barnyard chicken. He scratched the earth for worms and insects. He clucked and crackled, and he would thrash his wings and fly a few feet into the air. Years passed and the eagle grew very old. One day he saw a magnificent bird above him in a cloudless way. It glided in graceful majesty among the powerful wind currents with scarcely a beat of its wings. The old eagle looked up in awe. "Who's that," he asked? "That's the eagle, the king of birds," said his neighbor. "He belongs to the sky. We belong to the earth. We're chickens." So the eagle lived and died a chicken for that's what he thought he was.

This book is designed to transform us into eagles, away from "chicken-hood."

THE
?
BIG
QUESTION ?

Who is your worst enemy?

_____

_____

_____

Once you figure this out, the battle is almost won. I have discovered that you are the only person that can stop you from doing and being all that God would have for you to do and become. Here's the first rule of winning: Don't beat yourself.

The biggest enemy is you. When you find yourself getting in your own way, you're acting like an old refrigerator-it slowly builds an ice formation which, if allowed to accumulate unchecked, will reduce its effectiveness considerably.

"I have never met a man who has given me as much trouble as myself" (Dwight L. Moody)

How do you see yourself? Do you see and feel about your ministry the way the people who you are called to lead see and follow you?

We should never allow the world to see more potential in us to be used for their glory than we see in ourselves to be used for God's glory.

This truth is based on what we read in Exodus 4:10. Let's consider what Moses said about himself when The Lord wanted to use him to His glory. Now let's take a look at what the people in the Egyptian world that he was reared in had to say about him in Acts 7:20-22.

In Exodus 4:10, he said he could not speak. But in Acts 7:20, the Egyptians said he was learned in wisdom and he was mighty in words and deeds.

If we are going to be Effective Leaders and Pastors and Ministers who will rediscover the call, we must recognize that God is not interested in our ability, but our availability. God is able if we will only make ourselves available. Proverbs 18:16 A man's gift maketh room for him, and bringeth him before great men.

Prior to being selected by God for ministry leadership, and even since His choice of us, we all have so many things in common with Moses.

1. Many of us were running from the sins of our past. (Exodus 2:11-15)

2. We had a distinct call from God upon our lives. (Exodus 3:1-10)

3. It was an assignment that most of us did not welcome. (Exodus 3:11)

4. We were forced to deal with people who would not obey God's voice. (Exodus 3:13)

One way we rediscover the pastoral call and responsibility is we deal with what James Massey calls the burden and the joy of preaching the gospel.

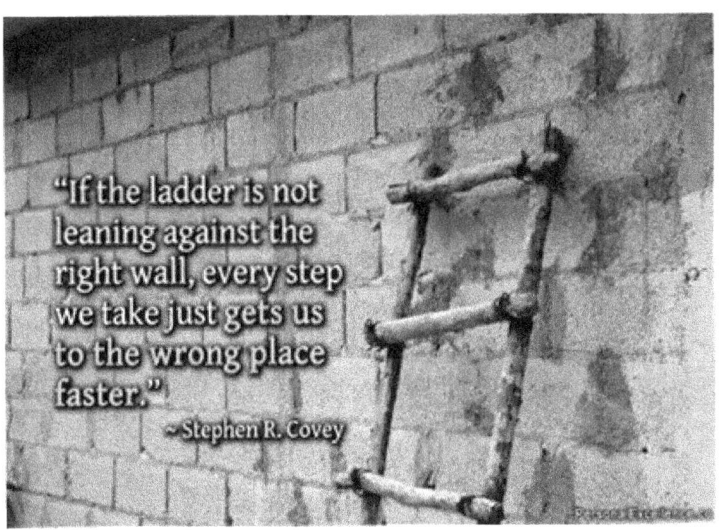

1 Peter 5: 2-5

Preachers and pastors are placed in a unique position every Sunday or every time they are called to share the word. Allow me to say at the outset of this discussion that it is a blessing and privilege to be able to preach. It is a privilege that should never be taken for granted. As a matter of fact, I will go as far as to say that preaching is the pastor's main responsibility. Notice one of Charles Spurgeon's Works Preaching Through Adversity. It was given in

1995 at Bethlehem Conference for Pastors By John Piper.

In 1995 John Piper said Everyone faces adversity and must find ways to persevere through the oppressive moments of life. I think we all can agree with that statement. Everyone must get up and make breakfast, wash clothes, and go to work, and pay bills, and discipline children and generally keep life going when the heart is breaking. But it's different with pastors--not totally different, but different. 1 Peter 5:2 clearly says We have been given the biblical charge to feed the flock not of ours but God which is among you.

So the question is or becomes what do you do when the preachers heart is broken?

The heart is the instrument of our vocation.

So when our heart is breaking we must labor with a broken instrument. I just wonder how many times have you had to take that long walk to your pulpit with a broken instrument? Some of you might be sitting here right now and your instrument is broken. With sins up on top of sins not of your congregation but your own. Preaching is our main work. And preaching is heart work, not just mental work.

So the question for us is not just how you keep on living when the marriage is blank, and a child has run away, and the finances don't reach, and pews are bare and friends have forsaken you; the question for us is more than, how do you keep on living? It's, How do you keep on preaching? How do you rediscover the call?

It's one thing to survive adversity; it is something very different to keep on preaching, Sunday after Sunday, month after month when the heart is overwhelmed. Spurgeon said to the students of his pastors' college, "One crushing stroke has sometimes laid the minister very low. Notice Spurgeon's words.

Just one blow has sometimes taken more out of you than all the licks you have ever taken.

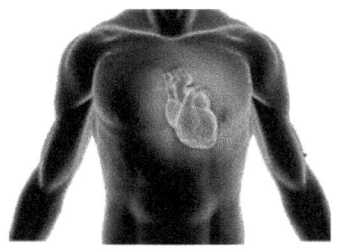

That blow, according to Spurgeon, is the brother most relied upon becomes a traitor...The sad reality of preaching and preachers is you don't know who you can trust and who you can share your heart with. The very reason why so many pastors are not here is because of a trust issue and a heart issue. Ten years of toil do not take so much life out of us as we lose in a few hours by Ahithophel the traitor, or Demas the apostate".

The question for us is not, how do you live through unremitting criticism and distrust and accusation and abandonment; for us the question is also, How do you preach through it?

How do you do heart work when the heart is under siege and ready to fall? How do you feed the flock of God which is among you? Preaching great and glorious truth in an atmosphere that is not great and glorious is an immense difficulty. Brothers unless you admit that fact, you failing to be real. It's hard to bake bread in a cold oven. To be reminded week in and week out that many people regard your preaching of the glory of the grace of God as hypocrisy pushes a preacher not just into the hills of introspection, but sometimes to the precipice of self-extinction.

I don't mean suicide. I mean something more complex. I mean

the deranging inability to know any longer who you are.

Many pastors have committed suicide.

Another church tragedy, Pastor Isaac Hunter—the son of the spiritual adviser to President Obama—has reportedly taken his own life. Hunter's death is making national headlines because of his megachurch father Pastor Joel Hunter's influence on the White House, his marriage troubles and an undated suicide note found last year, but his death is far from the only pastoral suicide in recent months.

Just days ago, a pastor who was grieving his dead wife reportedly shot himself in front of his mother and son, expressing that he was hearing his dead spouse's voice and footsteps. Pastor Ed Montgomery and his late wife, prophetess Jackie Montgomery, served at the Full Gospel Assemblies International church in Hazel Crest, Ill.

In November, a Georgia pastor killed himself in between Sunday services. Larrinecia Sims Parker, wife of the Rev. Teddy Parker Jr., found the pastor in the driveway of their home with a self-inflicted gunshot wound, Houston County coroner Danny Galpin reports.

According to the Schaeffer Institute, 70 percent of pastors constantly fight depression, and 71 percent are burned out. Meanwhile, 72 percent of pastors say they only study the Bible when they are preparing for sermons; 80 percent believe pastoral ministry has negatively affected their families; and 70 percent say they don't have a close friend.

What begins as a searching introspection for the sake of holiness and humility gradually becomes, for various reasons, a carnival of mirrors in your soul:

- You look in one and you're short and fat;

- You look in another and you're tall and skinny;

- You look in another and you're upside down.

And the horrible feeling begins to break over you that you don't know who you are any more. You have hidden behind so many masks that you don't know who you are or what direction you are going in. We wear the mask that grins and lies; it hides our cheeks and shades our eyes. This debt we pay to human guile; with torn and bleeding hearts we smile, and mouth with myriad subtleties.

Why should the world be over-wise, in counting all our tears and sighs? Nay let them only see us, while, we wear the mask.[3] Susan Howatch's book *Glittering Images*, recognizes through the skillful intervention of a wonderful spiritual director that he has been hiding behind a "glittering image."
What Glittering Image are you hiding behind?

_____

_____

The result is that his true self has not been allowed to unfold. As the spiritual director continues to guide him, he discerns how he uses the various skills and tools of his glittering image in his attempts to win the approval of others whereas his true self would rather be faithful in serving God without regard to others response.[4]

Brothers we I believe; no I know that we are tempted to hide behind our glittering images and hope that thereby others will approve of us. We may be asked to preach late-night; our name may be called on the big stage, all the while we would rather not acknowledge our broken selves, ourselves with problems, with secrets faults we would very much prefer everybody not to know.
The "Real" Preachers of Any City

A recent television show that was filled with glamour, glitz, and gold may have misrepresented the life of the preacher. While

---

[3] Paul Laurence Dunbar 1872-1906
[4] Peterson Eugene, Darwn Marva, The Unnecessary Pastor Rediscovering the Call, Regent College Publishing, pp. 24

there are pastors who have great ministries and very comfortable lifestyles, they are the exception and not the rule. I praise God for the awesome ministers who preach and lead in a dynamic way. Consequently, their ministries grow exponentially, and they are admired (and sometimes vilified) for their success.

What the show did not bring to light is the true cost of excellence and the difficult realities that come with ministry. Most pastors (especially very successful, high-profile pastors) struggle to balance their "blessedness" and their "brokenness." All pastors should agree – "Every day is NOT Sunday and Sabbath seems elusive!"

As pastors, we are grateful for the calling that God has placed on our lives and the joy of serving great people. However, few people ever see the pain in the average pastor's life. Simply put – a pastor's job is thankless, lonely, and agonizing. Rowland Crouch cites unrealistic expectations, multiplicity of roles, inability to produce 'win-win' conflict resolutions, administrative overload, and loneliness as reasons why at least one-third of pastors struggle with depression. Henri J. M. Nouwen calls today's clergy "wounded healers."

Though many people think the pastor works 30 minutes weekly, 90% of the pastors work 55 to 75 hours per week. What do pastors do? Sermon preparation, visitations, church administration, staff relations, community involvement, counseling, weddings, funerals, conflict resolution, worship planning, and the list goes on and on. This is in a mid-size or large ministry. Think about the pastors of smaller churches who open, close, and clean the church building. Those who type the bulletins, their sermons and other correspondence. With the average church in America only having about 60 members, most pastors have secular jobs in addition to the ministry. The pastor's job is NEVER done!

Be faithful! 80% of America's churches have less than 200 members (60% have less than 100 members). Even if God does not give you quantity, give him quality. You may never preach to thousands or preach on television but you and your ministry are significant in the eyes of our God and the people who love us. Keep the faith![5]

The theological problem that we are facing is the problem of the center.

The center is not holding. And if the center doesn't hold--if there is no fixed and solid "I" able to relate to the fixed and solid "Thou," namely, God, then who will preach next Sunday or better yet in the morning?

When the apostle Paul said in 1 Corinthians 15:10, "By the grace of God, I am what I am," he was saying something utterly essential for the survival of preachers in adversity.

If, by grace, the identity of the "I"--the "I" created by Christ and united to Christ, but still a human "I"--if that center doesn't hold, there will be no more authentic preaching, for there will be no more authentic preacher, but a collection of echoes.

Old wore out wore over sermons, and not a fresh word, a rhema word for this season.

However, thank God there is a cure and that cure is first operated in your authority.

Allow me to back and say that we have been given the charge to feed the flock of God, this is not our church, its God's church, these are not our people they are God's people. The business of the church is God's business. If God can't handle his business, it can't be handled. Go to sleep tonight knowing that God plus one is a majority.

How do we operate in our authority we take the oversight thereof?

Peter exhorts the leaders to shepherd their flock, by serving them before being served. In other words, become a minister to the

---

[5] Dr. R. Timothy Jones is pastor of the Peaceful Rest Missionary Baptist Church in Shreveport, Louisiana. He is former dean of the National Baptist Convention of America.

people. Ask yourself when I serve do I serve out of a sense of obligation or privilege?

Preachers catch more hell because they have given up their position of oversight over to a committee or a group of deacons or even to your bedroom at home, some spouses have more authority in the church than the pastor does. You give leadership to the flock or either you have surrendered your authority of oversight. Are you are a prophet or puppet? Who called you? Who commissioned you? Who are you trusting in, and leaning on?

The prophets remind Israel, just as we need to be reminded through a regular dose of prophetic preaching, that God is the sovereign creator and sustainer of the whole creation. The God who sent Jonah to preach salvation in Nineveh is the same God who used Babylon and Persia as the instruments of God's will.

The God who formed Israel into a great nation when they were delivered from bondage in Egypt is the same God who can send Israel back into captivity and cause them to hang their harps upon the willows and weep as they sit along the banks of the River Chebar and remember the life they once lived back in Zion.

God's concern is for the whole of creation and for all the people that dwell therein. When the people of God lose sight of the fact and begin acting as if only they and their nation really matter, it is time for a prophet to declare, "Thus says the Lord!" Not only do I see that we are called in this text to become ministers to the people. But I see that we should become mentors to the people. Not by constraint, but willingly. Peter asked them to willing invest, eagerly invest in the flock, not as lords, but as examples.

- Do you do first what you ask the people you lead to do? Are you being examples to your people?
- Do they see you giving?
- Do they see you investing in your family?
- Do they see you and your wife getting along?
- Do they see you loving your children?
- How do the men in the church see you?

- Do they see you peeping at their wife or girlfriend they bring to church or do they see you as a real man, a man that really loves The Lord?
- Do they see you as being an example for them to follow?

Not only do I see that we are called in this text to become ministers to the people, and not only do I see that we should become mentors to the people. But I also see that we should be both mangers and models for the people.

When you become a model you understand it's not about the money, the bible calls it filthy lucre, but you model with a ready mind.

A ready mind says send me I'll go…

A ready mind says here am I I'll serve even if I have to serve alone…

A ready mind says I will do your will even if I have to stand alone…

Because one day the chief Shepherd shall appear, and if you have stayed the course, and stayed in the race the bible says you shall receive a crown of glory that fadeth not away. The stuff you get for pastors anniversaries it will fade away

Those gator shoes will wear out

Those cuff links will rust away

That tailored made suit will on day rot away

But the crown of glory will not fade away

I'm so glad that my testimony is I got a crown up in that kingdom isn't that good news.

Reverend Dr. Jeffery A. Gladney

PART TWO : DEALING WITH THE PASTOR'S RESPONSIBILITY

Consider this illustration: While driving by an abandoned old church in Appomattox, VA and wondering what was their story? The Lord gave me the following statement. "They did not vote to die, they simply voted not to live." A beautiful little church in the vale out of the Norman Rockwell art gallery is now non-existent. The sad story was that no one in the neighborhood even knew their name. Now there is only a grassy knoll where the church once stood. I have pictures. I call it the church with no name.

THE
BIG
QUESTION?

How can you keep your church from becoming the church with no name? How can you revive your church?

-

_____

_____

_____

One way to keep your church from declining is start see things as Jesus saw them. (See John 4)

It's amazing what we don't see when we aren't looking! Learning to see from God's perspective was a teaching Jesus tried to drill home.

At the home of Simon the Pharisee, when the woman of the streets was lavishing adoring attention on Jesus, he posed the question to Simon: "Do you see this woman?" (Luke 7:44

emphasis added).

Religious people don't see people; they see causes, behaviors, stereotypes, and people other than them.

The reason why Jesus had trouble getting his disciples to see what he saw simply this: they had grown up in church! They had been trained to be concerned with internal issues rather than keeping their eyes on the harvest.

PART THREE : THE LAW OF CONNECTION

More than decades or centuries, history is marked by great ideas; that is, when someone, placed in unique culture and circumstance, stands up and says, "What if we believed-and acted upon-this?" Luther's idea of grace. Gandhi's idea of nonviolent resistance. Ford's idea of efficiency. Hitler's idea of nationalism. Einstein's idea of relativity. Jesus' idea of the church.[6]

Look with me in Jeremiah the 29th chapter. In this chapter I believe are effective strategies for rediscovering the pastoral call.

The city of Jerusalem was burned to the ground and the temple destroyed. The nation's leaders were dragged off as captives to the city of Babylon by the invading king Nebuchadnezzar. There in the city of their captors, these former Israelite leaders began to despair that God would ever deliver them.

How do you really feel about where your church is located and where God has you? What are you frustrated about concerning the ministry?

It was to those despairing, grieving captives that a letter came from the prophet Jeremiah. And his advice to those exiles is a word we need to hear as we seek to be God's faithful people in our time. That letter-and its advice-now appears in Jeremiah 29:4-13.

Notice that only when Babylon's seventy years are completed will I ...bring you back to (Jerusalem). You have to admit that Yahweh's initial promise to the Israelite political, economic, and religious leaders in Babylonian exile seems like a harsh promise.

Through this prophecy, God tells the Israelite leaders they

---

[6] Lewis Robert "The Church Of Irresistible Influence" Zondervan, Grand Rapids, Michigan, 2001

will remain in exile for seventy years-in others words a lifetime! They will not be restored to their precious city of Jerusalem. Likely neither will their children. Only in their grandchildren lies the hope that Israel will once again be restored to its land.

How then can God say to them, "I know the plans I have for you...plans for your (shalom) and not for your harm, to give you a future with hope"(Jeremiah 29:11)? What kind of future is God giving to them as they live and die in captivity? How is such a life of slavery "a future with hope" and free of "harm"?

Are you where you are by chance, circumstance or call?

In verse 7 Jeremiah tells them to "Seek the (Shalom) of the city where I have sent you into exile." The English word sent you into exile are actually the translation of a single Hebrew word that has double meaning. It can rightly be translated "exile" and it can also be translated "sent."

Thus it is reasonable to assume that in the use of this one Hebrew word, Jeremiah is seeking to communicate two distinct ideas to his Hebrew brothers and sisters in Babylon. He is, in essence, saying to the Israelites, "You are in captivity because your nation was defeated, your army destroyed, your city burned, and you were clapped into chains and marched across the desert into Babylonian exile.

That is your circumstance. But you are also in captivity because I, The Lord your God, sent you there. You are in Babylon because I need my people in this wicked county, or rural setting, or country road, or wherever you are. **That is your call from God.**[7]

You can't be effective in anyplace until you believe God has placed you there, for the people God has placed under you or with you!

---

[7] Linthicum Robert, Transforming Power, InnerVarsity Press, Downers Grove, Illinois, 2003

Here is God's promise--not only for Israelite captives but also for all of us called to be the church wherever we may be. We are not in our community simply because of our circumstances--because we were born there or moved there to take a job or to get an education or to accompany our spouse.

We are in this community because The Lord our God has called us there, sent us there and needs us there! We are in our location or town, mission station by the intentional will of God acted out through the particularity of our circumstances.

Therefore as God's sent people, what are we called to be and do in the place we are planted?

We are called to the very same task as were the Israelite captives in the city of Babylon twenty-six hundred years ago: (you are to) seek the (Shalom) of the place where you are planted, for in its (shalom) you will find your (Shalom) Jeremiah 24:7.

Note where we are to seek shalom. It is not in Jerusalem---the city of God. It is in Babylon-the city of Satan.

THE BIG QUESTION ? **What Is Shalom?**

Shalom is most often translated in to English as peace. But the Hebrew word shalom means much more than the simple cessation of hostilities. Shalom is an exceeding rich concept, a comprehensive word dealing with and covering all the relationships of daily life.

The fundamental meaning of shalom is captured by such English words as "Totality" "Wholeness" "Well-Being" and "Harmony." It is a comprehensive word that includes in it:

- Bodily health (Psalm 38:3)

23

- Security and Strength (Judges 6:23; Daniel 10:19)
- A long life ending in natural death (Genesis 15:15)
- Prosperity and abundance (Psalm 37:11)
- Successful completion of an enterprise (Judges 18:5)
- Victory in war (Judges 8:4-9)

So when Jews wish each other "shalom" they are wishing for each other health, security, long life, prosperity, successful completion, of an enterprise, victory in war.[8]

In other words, they are wishing God's best for the entirety of a person's life, for all her relationships with others, for all he sets his hand to do. And they are wishing for such fullness both for that person's life and for the Jewish community throughout the world.

Shalom captures the well-being of an entire society. The hope for you is to wish Shalom upon your community where you are planted.

How does this look in action?

- Become God's presence Jeremiah 29:5-6
- Pray for the setting where you are planted Jeremiah 29:7
- Practice your faith through action Jeremiah 29:7
- Proclaim the good news
1. First, we are to undertake ministries of mercy and seek to serve the needs of the poor.
2. Second, we are to be advocates for the powerless.
3. Third Community Development

Work in groups to develop a list of ministries or ideas under each category that will help us deal with our responsibility?

A young minister in a college town was embarrassed by the thought of criticism in his cultured congregation. He sought

---

[8] IBID

counsel from his father, an old and wise minister, saying: Father, I am hampered in my ministry in the pulpit I am now serving.

- If I cite anything from geology, there is Professor A, a teacher of this science, right before me.
- If I use an illustration of Roman mythology there is Professor B, ready to trip me up for my little inaccuracy.
- If I mention something in English literature that pleases me, I am cowered by the presence of the learned man that teaches that branch.

What shall I do?

The sagacious old man replied: Do not be discouraged, preach the gospel. They probably know very little of that.

I have decided to preach the gospel.

- The gospel that reaches the old in age and the young at heart.
- The gospel that reminds the saints of old to reach back and remember that when times get though and the going got rough: that old song that says "I've got a feeling everything's gone be alright. The Holy Ghost done told me everything's gone be alright,
- The gospel that reminds the young and the young at heart that weeping may endure for a night but Joy comes in the morning.
- I have decided to preach the gospel that reminds men, women, boys, and girls that the wages of sin is death but the gift of God is eternal life.
- I have decided to preach the gospel that reminds everyone that in Christ Jesus there are no big I's and little U's, Romans 3:23 says for all have sinned and fall short of the glory of God.

Preaching is the vehicle that God has chosen to introduce the world to a saving faith.

Paul in his letter to the church at Rome declared, "faith comes by hearing and hearing by the word of God." (Romans 10:17) 1 Corinthians 1:21 says For since, in the wisdom of God, the world through wisdom did not know God, it pleased God through the foolishness of the message preached to save those who believe.

The Greek word for preaching is kerygma, which means to proclaim the good news. 1 Corinthians 14:3 says But he who prophesies (preach) speaks edification and exhortation and comfort to men. This verse I believe gives us the foundation for biblical preaching.

Preaching should speak the language of the audience so that someone who hears the message can be built up and be encouraged. I pray that these God centered messages encourages your spirit in faith and love.

"AN INSPIRATIONAL LIGHTHOUSE STORY"

Many years ago, there was a little village on a rocky seacoast, where storms often battered, and seas were ever treacherous. Many ships were driven onto the rocks by the storms, and the lives of many sailors were lost because of the raging seas.

One day the people decided among themselves that they should establish a lighthouse and lifesaving station on a little peninsula on the coast, to warn ships away from the rocks and to save the lives of those who were cast into the icy waters. They approached the government and began to secure the necessary funds for their project. Soon they set forth and built a tower and set a beacon in it; they organized a lookout system; and they bought boats and learned how to man them; and soon they were in business. The business of saving lives!

Soon the effects of what they were doing became known far and wide. Fewer ships went on the rocks; and when such a tragedy did occur, and the alarm was sounded, the people risked their own lives to rescue those who had been cast into the raging, icy waters. Within a few short years, people came from great distance to study their lighthouse, and to use it as a model.

One day someone suggested that, since they all spent so much time at the lighthouse, they should gather there occasionally and enjoy good fellowship. And soon they began to get together (at first infrequently, and then more often) at the lighthouse. In fact, many people began to build their homes near the lighthouse. Then when the lookout sounded the alarm, they were there, ready to go out.

Next, it was decided that if they were going to spend so much time there, they must make the place more comfortable. So, arrangements were made to heat the lighthouse. The gray walls were painted a brilliant white. Some of the walls were paneled; rugs were put on the floors to disguise the bare concrete; a fine kitchen was installed with a handsome stove; and generally speaking, the lighthouse became a nice place to spend your time waiting for the alarm to be sounded. Everything about the lighthouse was made comfortable and nice. The lighthouse soon became the center of life in the little town that grew up around it.

One night a fierce storm blew in, as storms had blown in for years. Many ships were tossed on the jagged rocks, and the men at the lighthouse spent long hours picking sailors from the bitter cold icy waters and taking them to the lighthouse, where they were fed and provided with dry clothing. This had happened many times over the years, but this time, after the storm subsided and the sailors had all left the lighthouse, there were some men who were angry. It seems the storm had made them leave the comfort of the lighthouse, and go out into the wet, dangerous seas; and they got cold; very cold. The sailors, when they were delivered to the lighthouse, soiled the carpets. The kitchen was a mess, not to mention the stove. After a brief meeting it was first decided that sailors, when they were brought to the lighthouse, should be taken to the basement, not to the nice upper areas.

Sometime later, another storm blew in; and about one half of the men went out in the boats, and again picked sailors from the frigid waters. This time the ship, which had broken apart on the rocks, was from another nation; and the men who manned her spoke another language, and even worse were of a different color.

After this storm, a few more men joined those who refused to enter the sea. They decided that men like these did not belong in the lighthouse at all; some said they felt that the lighthouses' job was not supposed to be saving sailors from other lands, because they were so much different. There were those, too, who objected to leaving the comfort of the lighthouse to go out into the storm. These men petitioned the government and they also agreed. So, finally, it was decided that the beacon would be kept lit, but the rescue work would be discontinued.

A small group disagreed, however, and went down the coast, a short distance, and started a new lighthouse. This small group decided that they should establish the biggest lifesaving station on the little peninsula, and so they did. Every day they warned ships and sometimes attempted to save lives from the icy water. Fame of the new lighthouse grew and the lighthouse back up the bay eventually turned out its beacon.

Some people say the beacon can still be seen today in you and I. Oh yes, they also say the small group running the new lighthouse were those once rescued from the raging seas.

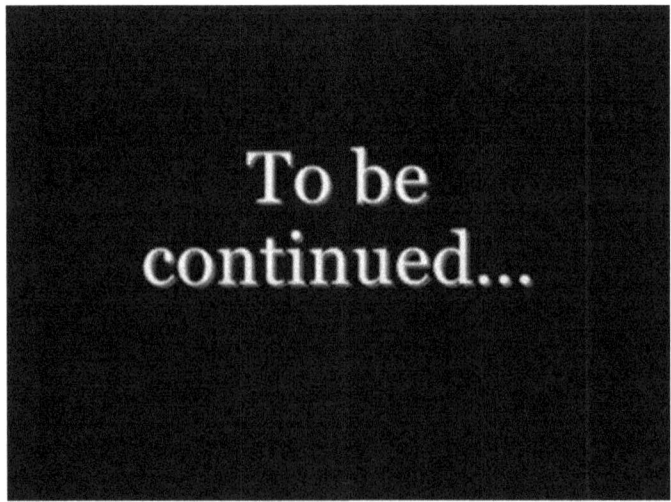

CHAPTER - SERMON FROM MARK 8

Reverend Dr. Jeffery A. Gladney

GOD WILL SUPPLY

Winne The Pooh said "the whole world is a series of miracles, but we're so used to them we call them ordinary things.

There are divine occurrences that have happened in our life that can only be described as a miracle. As a matter of fact, it was only because of God's Grace that you are still here today.

Our text of attention for today focuses on one of Jesus's miracles the feeding of the 4,000.

Here is another illustration of what Habershon calls "the double miracle," and much that we have written in connection with feeding the 5,000, which probably took place not far from the same scene as the miracle before us, is common to the feeding of the 4,000.

But I like to argue that the feeding of 5,000, and the feeding of 4,000 are two different miracles that occurred in two different places and on two different occasions.

The feeding of 4,000 is only found in Matthew and Mark's gospel, while the feeding of the 5,000 is found in all four gospels which makes it synoptic.

During the miracle of feeding the 5,000 the people followed Jesus one day, Matthew's gospel says it was a large crowd. The feeding of 4, 000 occurred after the people had been with Jesus over a three-day period of teaching and preaching. They had come to hear Jesus teach and the revival lasted three days.

If there is anything we need in this changing world of political unrest, hate filled rhetoric, wildfire burning, lack of love and unity in our communities, home, and churches is a soul stirring revival. Psalms 85:6 Wilt thou not revive us again: that thy people may rejoice in thee? In the feeding of the 5,000 there was a boy who had a snack lunch of two fish and five loaves of bread, when the 4,000 was fed the disciples brought 7 loaves and 7 fish. When the 5,000 was feed 12 baskets were left over, when the 4,000 was feed 7 basket was left over. Both miracles involved huge crowds.

- Both miracles involved huge crowds.
- Both miracles took place in a location where no food was available.
- In both miracles Jesus used a small amount of food to feed a lot of people.
- Both miracles involved the use of bread and fish.
- In both miracles Jesus involved the disciples. In one the disciples were unprepared and in the other they were under prepared.
- In both miracles the disciples doubted the Lord's ability to meet the need.
- In both miracles Jesus asked the question, "How many loaves have ye?" Jesus is not going to do for us what we can do for ourselves.
- In both miracles, Jesus took what He had, thanked God for it, and broke it.
- In both miracles the bread and fish multiplied in the hands

of Jesus.

- In both miracles the crowds were entirely satisfied.

- In both miracles a large amount of food was left over.

- While there are many similarities, there are also several differences between this miracle and the first.

- The amount of bread used in this miracle is different; 5 loaves verses 7 loaves.

In the first miracle Jesus was motivated by the spiritual needs of the crowd, Mark 6:34. In this miracle Jesus is motivated by the physical needs of the crowd.

The first miracle was performed using food from an outside source, John 6:9 you remember after a survey was taken a little boy had a snack lunch of two fish and five loaves. . In this miracle, it appears that Jesus used what the disciples already possessed.

The first miracle was designed to teach the disciples that Jesus was "the Bread of Life" for the Jews. This miracle is designed to teach them that Jesus is "the Bread of Life" for the world. Philippians 2:10 That at the name of Jesus every knee should bow, of things in heaven, and things in earth, and things under the earth; Philippians 2:11 And that every tongue should confess that Jesus Christ is Lord, to the glory of God the Father.

Notice first of all, the occasion and motive in the two miracles were different. Also in the miracle of the 5,000, the disciples spoke first, while in that of the 4,000 Jesus takes the initiative. Let's unpack this day after revival when 4,000 people sat on grass that would later be burned up. The Bible says a great multitude of

Gentiles from the region of Decapolis followed Jesus into a desert place, they were attracted by His unique and marvelous teaching they remained with him for three days.

Mark 8:4 And his disciples answered him, From whence can a man satisfy these men with bread here in the wilderness? Notice the pace of this revival was in a desert place-a desert place is a place of little to no provision. God majors in dealing with desert places in our physical and spiritual lives. Do you remember the time when you had more month than money and you were able to make it anyhow. That was God leading you through your desert place. Do you remember the time sickness was abound in your body the doctor said one thing but after prayer and you trusting in the Lord, God said another thing...That was God leading you through your desert place.

Do you remember the time the person who said they would be by your side forever one day walked out on you and left you left but you still standing, still in your right mind, still got your joy that was God leading your desert place......

If you came in and it seem like life has you in a place of no provision or little provision then you in the right place for a miracle to occur in your life. Notice again that the conversation in Mark's gospel is started not by the disciples but by Jesus.

Mark 8:1 In those days the multitude being very great, and having nothing to eat, Jesus called his disciples unto him, and saith unto them, Mark 8:2 I have compassion on the multitude, because they have-now been with me three days, and have nothing to eat:

Aren't you glad that we serve a God who is compassionate and merciful and knows when we have a need just by looking at us.

Jesus after three days' notice something as the service was ending. Mark 8:3 And if I send them away fasting to their own houses, they will faint by the way: for divers of them. came from far. Jesus is always in the business of meeting your needs. Jesus has always been by your side. Jesus has always stood by you even when it seems like you were standing all by yourself, you were never alone.

A woman was at home alone one day and man tried to rob her and she started screaming Acts 2:22, Acts 2:22. T her surprise the man took off running. The cops later caught the man and they asked him why did he run. His response was the lady said she had an, ax and two twenty-twos. The Lord is always watching over you.

Jesus desire is to help you in whatever situation you are face it. The disciples came to the conclusion after Jesus ask the question was a confession of insufficiency of their own resources to cope with the need. They had no supply for such an emergency. Have you been there where you know you had a need but you did not know how the need was going to be met. The disciples just like us has a short memory because they had just witnessed the feeding of the 5,000. They should have known if God did it before he can do it again. God may have divided the Red Sea of Israel yet no sooner are they on the other side, they complain and forget.

They later asked for water and he brought water from a rock.

When we think about what God brought us out of the last time it out to give us the assurance that God can bring us out again. Somebody shout Lord do it again. Make a way out of no way again, heal gain , Deliver again, take little and make much out of it gain.

Take care of the school year again

Take care of my frailties and faults again

Take care of my shortcomings again

Jesus ask what do you have available for the people. Mark 8:5 And he asked them, How many loaves have ye? And they said, Seven. In other words they did not even have enough food for themselves. Jesus says tell the people to sit down. Mark 8:6 And he commanded the people to sit down on the ground: and he took the seven loaves, and gave thanks, and brake, and gave to his disciples to set before them; and they did set them before the people.

Notice Jesus here did the same thing he did in the communion meal he took and blessed, broke it and gave it to his disciples and said give to the people. Mark tell us that first He gave thanks for the bread, and afterwards blessed the fishes. Notice that after the blessing the food supply never ran out.

This lesson teaches us that when and whatever we put in God's hand becomes more than enough to supply our physical and spiritual need. As a matter of fact they sent out seven basket and took up seven baskets. Wait don't miss your shout they sent out seven basket and took up seven basket. Mark 8:8 So they did eat, and were filled: and they took up of the broken meat that was left seven baskets. How can you feed that many people and still have the same number of baskets of food left over? As a matter of fact the Bible says it was seven large basket of leftover.

Whatever you give to Jesus is not in vain. And when you give it get ready for a equal or greater return. Let's do some biblical math seven is the number of perfection, seven repeated twice is the sign of a double blessing. Because they had seven loaves and seven fish-that's double seven. Not only that we see the number 4 which is symbolic of the Lord opening his of compassion for the whole world not just a select few. This miracle lets us know that if we have a need Jesus has the supply. When I think about the Goodness if Jesus and all he has done for me my soul cry hallelujah thank you God for saving me. Has the Lord done anything for you that you know you could not have done for yourself. If He has that was a miracle. When the doctor say no and God say yes that was a miracle. When friends and family walk out on you and you sill made it that was nothing but a miracle. When you came out of your situation and you know had it not been for God you would not be here that was nothing but. Miracle.

When Christ came to earth He found our

Thirst, and He quenched it

Hunger, and He satisfied it

Shame, and He removed it

Trouble and He cured It

Loss, and He returned it

Turmoil, and He calmed it

And He Found our debt and He paid it…..paid it in full….

Tell your neighbor you looking at a miracle, a walking, talking, running, shouting, never doubting miracle….I just don't look like what I been through. God done so much for me you can't me doubt Him. You can't shake my faith.

KEEP MOVING

Mark 8:13 reads, "And he left them, and entering into the ship again departed to the other side." A truck driver was taking his load to a new destination. As he drove, he was intently watching the signs leading to his exit. In his effort to find the right exit, he missed the signs warning him of a low overpass ahead.

To his astonishment, his truck became stuck under the overpass. He could not go forward and he could not back up. Traffic began to back up and tempers began to flare. The police were called, wreckers were summoned, and an effort began to free the stuck truck.

They tried tow trucks, wenches, grease, pulleys, wedges and anything else anyone suggested. Nothing worked. The hours passed and the truck remained just as stuck as ever.

By this time a considerable crowd had gathered to watch the workers in their attempts to free the truck. In that crowd was a little boy who was riding his bicycle over the overpass. He had stopped to watch the show, and after a few minutes, he called out to one of the policemen below.

He said, "Hey officer, I know how to get that truck out from under that bridge."

The policeman looked up, but ignored the little boy.

The boy, wanting to help, cried out louder, "Hey officer, I know how to get that truck out from under that bridge."

With a hint of irritation in his voice, the police officer said,

"Okay young man, tell me how."

Without a pause, the little boy said, "Let some of the air out of the tires."

That's what they did and the truck was able to pull free.

I don't know if that tale is true or not, either way the story does teach a couple of important truths. First, it's easy to overlook the obvious, even when it is staring you right in the face. Second, wise people learn to pay attention to all the signs. Signs are important in this physical world. I have missed a few turns because I missed a road sign. I have been speeding because I missed a sign that told me to slow down. Signs help you to know where you are and what you are supposed to be doing. Signs serve a valuable purpose in our lives.

Just as there are signs in the physical realm, there are also signs in the spiritual arena. Those signs are even more important than the signs in the physical world. An alive church pays attention to the signs God is showing us.

You can miss a sign or two here and things will probably turn out fine. But, if you miss too many spiritual signs, you might end up in Hell. At the very least, you will end up in deep trouble with the Lord.

This passage tells us about a group of people who missed all the signs and got themselves into big trouble with the Lord Jesus. Let's watch what happens when you miss the spiritual signs the Lord has prepared for you.

Jesus has just finished one of the greatest miracles of His ministry. He took seven small loaves of bread and a few small fish and He fed four thousand people. When the meal was over, the disciples collected seven baskets filled with leftovers from the meal. According to verse 10, Jesus and His men immediately leave by ship and go to another part of Israel.

Mark 8:11 "And the Pharisees came forth, and began to question with him, seeking of him a sign from heaven, tempting him." As soon as they arrive there, they are met by the Pharisees. You might remember that the Pharisees were the religious conservatives of their day. They were very legalistic and they hated Jesus because He refused to do things the way they said things were supposed to be done.

When Jesus arrives in their neck of the woods, they came out to meet Him. The Bible says, in verse 11, that they "began to question with Him". The word "question" means "to dispute or argue" and the word is in a tense that suggests they wouldn't shut up. They kept on trying to drag Jesus into a theological argument.

Be careful around folk who only want to argue about the Bible but you never see them reading the Bible or studying the Bible. Some folk majors in drama and church conflict and not in love and unity.

We are told what they were trying to get Jesus to do. They wanted Him to show them "a sign from Heaven". The Bible says that they were "tempting Him". That is, they were putting Him to the test. They were trying to get Jesus to prove His authority and the source of His Power.

Notice they wanted Jesus to put on a show, work some magic, Lord if it's you and you have all power prove it. After all, if Jesus is of God, the Son of God, then surely He could do some wonder in the sky above to prove it. Other men of God had done similar things in Israel's past.

- Joshua had commanded the sun to be still and it had obeyed, Josh. 10:12-14.
- Samuel prayed during a battle and the Lord answered with strong and loud thunder which confounded and discombobulated their enemies.
- Elijah prayed and it did not rain for three and one-half years, 1 Kings 17:1. He prayed again and it rained, 1 Kings 18:41-45. Elijah also called down fire from the heavens which consumed a sacrifice and the altar it lay upon, 1 Kings 18:36-38.
- Others had done similar things in the past to prove that they were from the Lord.

What these men were really trying to do was to get Jesus to promise more than He could deliver. They knew about the things He had done with people, demons and food. They were trying to get Him to attempt a miracle and fail so that they could denounce Him as a false prophet.

They were also saying that all the things Jesus had already

done in the power of God were insufficient to prove that He was the Messiah. They knew the things He had done, but they wanted more!

How can you look at all the Lord has done in your life and say you need another sign? If the Lord does not do anything else for you He has already done enough?

Consider all the miracles the Jews had already witnessed.

- Jesus had healed the sick.
- He had raised the dead.
- He had delivered people from the bondage of demon possession.
- Jesus had walked on water.
- Jesus had calmed storms.
- Jesus had twice multiplied a meager amount of food and fed vast multitudes with it. On one occasion he feed 5,000 on another occasion he feed 4,000.
- Jesus had opened the Word of God, preached it clearly and made the-meaning of the Scriptures plain to all who heard Him.

The people were all talking about Him. They said "We never saw it on this fashion", Mark 2:12. They said, "He hath done all things well" Mark 7:37.

The Pharisees had heard enough Gospel to save the world. They had seen enough proof to convince the most stubborn of skeptics. Their problem was simply that they did not want to believe on Jesus! They did-not want Him to be their Messiah. They refused to bow to Him as their Savior!

Their problem is just like the modern day church's problem. They refuse to submit to the power of God until tragedy hit their life personally. We still have the Pharisees with us today. We still have the people who demand to see something sensational before they will commit to following Jesus. People thrive on the sensational. People flock to whatever church they fill will offer them the sensational one minute they at Red Oak, the next minute they up the street at another church because that church promises them the sensational. No commitment, no loyalty, people are not looking unto Jesus, they looking unto the sensational.

Far too many people are waiting on some supernatural event to prove the existence of God. The fact is, God has already proven that He exists!

While the world is looking for a sign, God tells us that He is visible in the ordinary things of this world. The things we take for granted every day are the very things that prove God is real. Let me share a few with you.

Consider the heavens; Psalm 19:1-4 God tells us that the heavens above tell us about Him.

- Our earth is traveling around its own axis at 1000 m.p.h.
- It moves around the sun at 67,000 m.p.h.
- It is carried by the sun across our galaxy at a speed of 64,000
- m.p.h.

- It moves in orbit around our galaxy at 481,000 m.p.h.
- It travels through space at 1,350,000 m.p.h.
- Every twenty-four hours we cover 57,360,000 miles.
- Each year we travel 20,936,400,000 miles across empty space.
- And every movement in the billions of galaxies in the universe occurs with precise, split-second timing.

I say again If the Lord does not do anything else he has already done enough. Mark 8:12 And he sighed deeply in his spirit, and saith, Why doth this generation seek after a sign? verily I say unto you, There shall no sign be given unto this generation. Notice the words of the text and He Sighed deeply When you look at the word sigh etymologically you notice when sigh is used as a verb a it means to:

1. emit a long, deep, audible breath expressing sadness, relief, tiredness, or a similar feeling. "Harry sank into a chair and sighed with relief"

When sigh is used as a noun it suggest

1. a long, deep, audible exhalation expressing sadness, relief, tiredness, or a similar feeling. "she let out a long sigh of despair.

When the text says Jesus Sighed deeply in his spirit - it suggests His heart was deeply affected at their wickedness and hypocrisy. The word "spirit" here is taken as the seat of the emotions, passions, affections. He drew groans deeply from his breast. And he sighed deeply in his spirit—The language is very strong.

This verse lets us get a glimpses into the interior of the Redeemer's heart, in which our Evangelist abounds, are more precious than rubies. The state of the Pharisaic heart, which prompted this desire for a fresh sign, went to His very soul.

And he sighed deeply in his Spirit. In his human soul; and which shows that he had one, and was subject to grief and sorrow, and all passions and infirmities, excepting sin.

This deep sigh was on account of the hardness of their hearts, the malignity of their minds, and insincerity of their intentions, who had no view to come at truth by this inquiry, but to ensnare him. He sighed deeply in His spirit: This attack and the unbelief it showed distressed Jesus. He was amazed at the unbelief and audacity of these religious leaders. "The sigh was physical, its cause was spiritual – a sense of irreconcilable enmity, invincible unbelief, and coming doom." (Bruce) This demand for a "special" sign was an extreme example of the arrogance and pride of the Pharisees towards Jesus. Essentially, they said, "You have done a lot of small-time miracles. Come on up to the big leagues and really show us something."

Sometimes the only thing you can do is sigh. When you look at the events of the world it should cause you to sigh.

Of all the issues with Gun violence. Mississippi has the nerve to have a tax free weekend on gun sales. That along ought cause you to sigh. Of all the mass shooting, police shooting, school shooting, and Mississippi has a tax-free 2nd Amendment gun sale weekend. When Welfare money was supposed to go to poor and needy families-But Brett Fave and Tate Reeves took that money and built a volley Ball court, and hired a personal trainer for the Governor-it ought to cause you to sigh…

When you saw Tricky, traitor Trump get a 200,000 bail, walk in the Fulton County jail and walk out and get back on his private plane with no jail time and you got countless black and brown people spending years behind bars for far less crimes…It ought to make you sigh..

Jesus looks and sighs…

Well when you look at the condition of the church and state of the church I am sure it causes you to sigh…You can't get ten people to come to Sunday School and less than that to Bible Study. It ought to cause you to sigh… Church Attendance is down universal not because of COVID But because of convictions, Apathy, Lack of concern for the things of God-it ought to cause you to sigh, and groan deeply in your spirit…

One Sunday you here three Sundays you gone—-and it don't bother you to the point of feeling bad…..that alone ought to cause you to sigh. When Jesus see the giving pattern of today's church it causes him to sigh deeply. What makes you sigh? Chasing the bottom of the bottle and it keep leaving you empty. Smoking weed and never getting satisfied.

Running from man to man or woman to woman and still lonely Putting all your energy and effort into pleasing other instead of pleasing God… What is it that causes you to groan in your spirit… Jesus looks at them and says, "No sign shall be given to this generation: Jesus refused because His miracles are not done with the intention of convincing hardened unbelievers.

Jesus is not in the business of preforming for your satisfaction… Instead, Jesus did miracles to show the power of God in the context of mercy. Those who believe that if people see enough signs they will come to faith presume to know more than Jesus did. He condemned the generation who sought a sign. You don't want church service not to last too long, preacher-preacher me happy, and don't bother my sins and my convections, but leave me feeling good about living in sin, don't tell me that if I don't get right my foot might slip and I end up in hell. Mark 8:12 And he sighed deeply in his spirit, and saith, Why doth this generation seek after a sign? verily I say unto you, There shall no sign be given unto this generation. Then Jesus says why are you asking for a sign after all the signs you missed.

He expostulates with them upon this demand; "Why doth this generation seek after a sign; this generation, that is so unworthy to have the gospel brought to it, and to have any sign accompanying it; this generation, that so greedily swallows the traditions of the elders, without the confirmation of any sign at all; this generation, into which, by the calculating of the times prefixed in the Old Testament, they might easily perceive that the coming of the Messiah must fall; this generation, that has had such plenty of sensible and merciful signs given them in the cure of their sick? What an absurdity is it for them to desire a sign!

What more do you want after all God has already done for you? The Lord been good to you what more do you want? The Lord been better to you then you been to yourself what more did you want.

> You have a roof over your head….
>
> Your shoes on your feet
>
> You have clothes on your back
>
> You have food to eat
>
> You have a car to get you from point a to b
>
> You have the activities of your limbs
>
> You have a piece of your mind left
>
> You have family and loves one doing fine
>
> Your children are ok

You have a church that brought up your grandmother, took in your mother, now training your children, and you want come….What more of a sign can the Lord give you……

What more can God do…..

He refuses to answer their demand; Verily, I say unto you, there shall no sign, no such sign, be given to this generation.

When God spoke to particular persons in a particular case, out of the road of his common dispensation, they were encouraged to ask a sign, as Gideon and Ahaz; but when he speaks in general to all, as in the law and the gospel, sending each with their own evidence, it is presumption to prescribe other signs than what he has given.

Shall any teach God knowledge? He denied them, and then left them, as men not fit to be talked with; if they will not be convinced, they shall not; leave them to their strong delusions. Next time someone try to argue with you about the things of God do like Jesus…..Can I show you what Jesus did Mark 8:13 And he left them, and entering into the ship again departed to the other side.

Jesus did not argue with them he kept moving and stayed focused on his purpose… Jesus knew that no good could come from further dialogue with them Jesus left them and again departed to the other side… Jesus knew who he was and whose he was… I learned an important lesson from Jesus as he was getting into the ship to leave… Help me preach tell your neighbor I'm stingy with me… not everyone deserve my time, not ever situation deserve my energy, not ever conversation deserve my input, not everyone deserve me… so I am going to keep moving… until your energy matches mine… your vision matches mine… your desire for the things of God line up with the word of God… I am going to keep moving

There are some places that I am going to move past There are some people I am going to move past it's not that I am better than they are, it's just that they not trying to go where the Lord is taking me……

Learn how to keep moving!

First Rule of Mental health learn to distinguish who deserves an explanation who deserves only one answer-and who deserves absolutely nothing…

- Doubt see the obstacle -faith see the way-keep moving
- Doubt sees the darkest night-faith see the day-keep moving slide

There is a picture of a chess game hanging in Paris. On one side of the painting is the Devil, and on the other side is a lad about sixteen years of age. They are playing chess. The Devil has a leering, triumphant expression on his face. He has just licked this boy at chess, and the boy is sitting there with his head bowed and big tears trickling down his cheeks. The Devil has just won in the game of life over this lad. He has no strength, he has no way out, and he has given up. The title of the picture is "Check Mate". He had him.

A famous chess player came through one day. He looked at the painting. He felt sorry for the boy and he hated the looks of the Devil. He began to study the board where the men were placed, and all of a sudden he shouted: "Son, I have found a move, one move. If you will make that move you can lick the Devil." He forgot himself, he forgot it was a painting-he was so engrossed in it.

- No matter what life has thrown you, you still have one move left.
- No matter what situation you are facing you still have one move left……..

- There was a man who taught us how to keep moving
- He moved down through forty-two generations kept moving
- He moved from heaven to earth through a Virgin named Mary
- He moved from Mary's body to a stable where he was born in Bethlehem
- He moved from a stable to teaching in temple when he was twelve
- He moved from teaching at twelve to opening blind men eyes and deaf men ears,
- He moved from there to causes the lame to walk and dumb to talk
- He moved from there to being accused of being the king of jews he moved from court room to courtroom and being falsely accused…..he moved from the courtroom to cross…He kept moving
- From the courtroom he moved to Calvary He kept moving
- He was nailed to the cross,
- He was lifted up on the cross and moved from the cross the grave and his last move he made was from the grave the sky.
- He now seated at the right hand of the father pleading my case.
  - He has all power in his hand.

A SECOND TOUCH

Many of you I am sure have heard the name Isaac Newton: in science he developed Newtons laws of motion.

Newton was undoubtedly a genius when it came to math, but he had some failings early on. He never did particularly well in school and when put in charge of running the family farm, he failed miserably, so poorly in fact that an uncle took charge and sent him off to Cambridge where he finally blossomed into the scholar we know today. He failed at first but succeed the second time around notice the text and you will see a similar story.

The gospel of Mark is the only one that records this particular story. It's not housed in Matthew, Luke or John.

The Bible says they came to Bethsaida, Bethsadia location" is important it is strategic stop, geographically it is located in the northeast corner of the sea of Galilee near where the Jordan River flows into it.

Bethsaida names means in Hebrew the house of the fisherman.

The Apostle Peter, Andrew, and Philip were born there. However Bethsadia was one of the cities also that at one point that was cursed for not accepting Jesus. (Matthew 11:21-22, Luke 10:13-14) now Jesus and his disciples stop by Bethsaida one more time.

That statement within itself suggest good news for the unbeliever, and for those who did not accept Jesus at first. Jesus is so compassionate that he will stop by the same place more than once. He will keep knocking at the door of your heart until you answer.

Don't give up on God, He will not give up on you.

The center piece of the Gospel narrates the journey of Jesus and the disciples from the northern most point in Palestine, southward to Jerusalem.

This mission from Caserea Philippi in Northern Galilee to Jerusalem is more about the disciples and Jesus teaching them about his identity or christiology and leading them in the way of discipleship, discipleship is what it means to follow Jesus.

Jesus was so concerned about the disciple that he wanted them to really understand what it mean to be a part of the kingdom, be a part of the church, be a part of Christianity. So he taught them not in the classroom but in the laboratory, this was hands on teaching 101.

Jesus notice that while he is teaching them that the disciples has a problem because he has to tell them in verse 15 beware of the yeast of Pharisees and the yeast of Herod. The Pharisees in verse 11 wanted Jesus to give them a sign from heaven to test Jesus and Jesus called them a previous generation and told them no sign would be given to that generation.

We asked you last week what more do you want to see after all the Lord has already done in your life. The disciples said did he compare us to the Pharisees because we have no bread. The disciples here appear a little slow. They act like they just don't get it. How many times has The Lord blessed you and you turn around and act like the Pharisees and the disciples at this point? Jesus just finished feeding four thousand people that were following him with seven loaves of bread in a desert, with a few small fish, and seven basket from a snack lunch was taken up. How can you turn around ask is Jesus talking about bread when he is the bread of life? How can they not have joy when they are walking and talking with the Joy of life? How can they be devoid of meaning when they are walking with the one who has all knowledge and power within himself? Before the story turns and you tune me out we do the same thing in the church and in life. We receive blessing after blessing and we turn around and doubt the God of our salvation just because a little trouble comes our way.

The same God of yesterday is the same God of our today. If God did it before he can do it again. If he brought you out before he can bring you out again. So we arrive in Mark symbolically at the place of Bethsida. This text is first tailored to teach us about the importance of evangelism and friendship. Its right before your very eyes in plain sight. Some people brought a blind man to him and begged him to touch him. This text suggest that these unnamed people where friends of this blind man whose name we don't know.

These people had enough sense to bring this man to Jesus. They were evangelistic enough to go and bring him to church because they knew him personally. They knew his back story. They felt sorry for him or better yet had Godly compassion on him. You have a nice car outside full of gas, or maybe somewhere between full and empty, and plenty of room in your vacuum and washed car and you know of plenty people personally that are hurting and you did not think to stop with your big fine automobile to pick up any of them.

An alive church is a church that brings people to Christ.

An alive church focuses on Evangelism inside the walls and outside the walls.

Allow me to pull over long enough to say that The Van Ministry should never stop picking up people to make sure they are able to come to church. These people brought this blind man to Jesus. Nine-five percent of people who come to Christ were brought by a friend who is saved. It is September, the ninth month of the year of 2023, ask yourself have, I invited, or better yet brought anybody to Church with me this year. You have had 8 months 243 days to invite someone to church. If you looked back at the start of this year and bringing someone to church has not been on your agenda Shame on you. If not, you are failing to do your job as a disciple of Christ.

Notice the text the friends brought this man and they did not stop there they begged Jesus to touch him. They besought, Jesus they had heard about the wonder working miracles of Jesus. Maybe thy heard about the man that was healed of leprosy. Maybe they heard about the woman with the issue of blood that touched the hem of his garment and was healed. Maybe they had heard about how Jesus healed Peter mother-in-law! Maybe they had heard about the Syrophoenician woman whose daughter was vexed with a demon that Jesus healed. Maybe they heard about the power of Jesus to feed a larger number of people with just fish and loaves.

But whatever the case is they are found on this day begging Jesus for a cure. Since you got up this morning, and you made your way to the church house, I just wonder is there anything you need to beg for, I am not talking about man but ask Jesus for?

Does anybody have anything that they need, if so the Bible tells us to ask, seek, and knock and the door will be opened unto us. I have news for you and that news is the healer is here, the way maker is present right now and he is excited to heal you. Not only does this text shows us a picture of evangelism and friendship: but This text is also tailored to teach us that Jesus sometimes has to move us away from some people in order to heal us.

This text moves Jesus from the crowd to a personal encounter.

Micklem says that, Apparently those who brought him thought it was only necessary for Jesus to touch him in order to regain his sight. (8:23) But Jesus was not a miraculous therapeutic machine: he dealt with individuals, individually and personally and not in a mechanical way. Aren't you glad that Jesus is concerned about your personal issue. Luke 12:7 Indeed, the hairs of your head are all counted. Don't be afraid; you are worth more than many sparrows!

1 Peter 5:7 casting all your care on Him, because He cares about you. Because of the friends the blind man has Jesus full attention. Notice the movement of the text Jesus personally takes

the blind man by the hand and led him outside the village. This miracle occurred because of the friends but it was now about the man and his faith and not for everybody else to know. There are some things that only Jesus can do for you. I keep saying this next level is not for everyone, everybody can't handle what's about to happen your life. Because you don't have the same stuff going on in your life that somebody else has, it might be similar but its not the same. At some point you and Jesus got to get outside of your normal village and you have to trust in Jesus even if you can't see where he is guiding you.

The man could not see because he is blind, he knew he had to be led and willing to follow if he was going to get his sight back. The movement of the text get strange because the man and Jesus are outside of the village and Jesus stops at a certain point and spit on the man eyes, and put his hands on Him. Wait notice the text again, and when he had spit on his eyes, this is strange even for a time with non-medical advancement. Charles Spurgeon said this strange act brought Jesus under ordained but despicable means.

They are in a place that is near water because I told you that the name of the city was Bethsaida which means in Hebrew the house of the fisherman. Why Jesus could you not have walked a little further and just put water on the man eyes if you wanted them to get wet rather than spit in his face. Well the answer was not apparent at first but I dug a little bit and found an answer. This stage of the miracle was the application of moisture from our Lord's mouth to the eyes of the blind man.

Here as J. N. Darby put it, "Jesus uses that which was of Himself, that which possessed the capability of His own person to perform the cure. In other words Jesus used something on the inside of himself that was a part of himself. Spittle in connection with the sanctity of the rabbis, was highly esteemed by the Jews in this respect; but here its virtue is connected with the Person of Him who used it? Salvia was reckoned to be a remedy for blindness. Jesus does thing outside the box, your miracle may not come in some traditional way, or in some normal method. If you sick and tired of being sick and tired you will say Jesus anyway you bless me I will be satisfied even if you have to spit in my face.

(Somebody shout bless me Lord anyway you choose.)

Bless me Lord anyway you choose to bless me. Notice the text after the spit here is where it gets even more interesting. After the spit Jesus lays his hands on the man's eyes and asked him a question Can you see anything? This is the first time we hear the man speak he says I see people, but they look like trees, walking.

This suggest to me that the man had not been born blind. Although he knew they were men he saw, he could not discern the shape and magnitude of the objects before him. This sounds just like the Pharisees and the disciples at this point, or better yet this sounds like church folk. You see God at work but you act like you just got off the short bus. Don't discount the blessing of the Lord because you want let some stuff go. Don't miss your miracle focusing on your mess. Use those eyes to see the goodness of the Lord. Use those ears to hear the joy of Jesus blessings. Use those hands to bless God with.

The Message Bible says it this way in verse sixteen, Meanwhile, the disciples were finding fault with each other because they had forgotten to bring bread. 18 Jesus overheard and said, "Why are you fussing because you forgot bread? Don't you see the point of all this? Don't you get it at all? The New Revised Standard Version says " Do you have eyes, and fail to see? Do you have ears, and fail to hear? And do you not remember? Does anybody remember what the Lord really brought you out of? Do you remember when you really encountered the Lord in a real way.

The blind man first touch is symbolic of the disciples lack of understanding of Jesus's mission and what he was sent to do. They have walked with Jesus, prayed with Jesus, and talked with Jesus and they act like they just didn't understand. There are people who you know if it had not been for The Lord they never would have made it. You know for yourself: If had not been for The Lord you would have been dead a long time ago. I mean you see the church progressing, you see the people of God being blessed, you see the hand of God upon the people of God and you still don't get it. 120 years and the church still standing… still saving souls, still giving hope in this lost world… still mission minded… still focused on caring about each other… still standing on the promises of God.

This text is tailored to teach us that Jesus will do it again! So this is what Jesus did for the blind man, the Bible says in verse 25 Then Jesus laid his hands on his eyes again: Again-is defined as another time, or once more. Again for the sake of this sermon is defined as the Second Touch. Notice what happened to this man after the second touch. This man the Bible says and he looked intently and his sight was restored, and he saw everything clearly.

This man blindness was symbolic of the churches spiritual blindness. If you continue to tip and not tithe you need a second touch. If you continue to fail to see how good God is to Red Oak Grove you need a second touch. If you keep doing things your way and not God's way you need a second touch. This man had to have a second touch just like us if we don't continue to recognize the goodness of The Lord in a real way. This man now is told to go back home, but go a different way. Jesus said don't go back even into the village. The village is where unbelievers are go home where some folk at who know your real story, your back page story and when they ask you what happened you can Give Glory to God and say I Received A Second Touch From The Master.

If your testimony is The first touch wasn't good enough because I went back out into the world. Don't act like you been that way your whole life. You haven't always looked that good, and shouted that much. Notice this man's back story:

I thought I knew what I was doing, I changed dance partners I stop dancing in the church and started dancing in the club. I thought I knew what I was doing. I stop drinking communion juice and started drinking Gin-n-Juice. I stopped singing amazing grace and started singing *Now Do That Nay-Nay-Now Do The Wip.* But something happened to me one day. But something happened to me one day. Jesus came by and Touched Me A Second Time. Jesus

Came by and touched me again. Jesus came by and touched me once more. This time I am going to praise God for my new touch. My new testimony is now I looked at my hands and they look new after my Second Touch. I looked at my feet and they look different after my Second Touch. The places I use to go I don't have a desire to go there anymore after my Second Touch. The Hymn writer said:

He touched me, oh He touched me
And oh the joy that floods my soul
Something happened and now I know
He touched me and made me whole.

As a Matter of fact it was the Second Touch that made a difference:

Since I met the blessed Saviour
Since He cleansed and made me whole
I will never cease to praise Him
I'll shout it while eternity rolls.

Does anybody need a second touch? Does anybody need to tell The Lord to do it again?

DO YOU KNOW HIM FOR YOURSELF

Mark 8 has been the backdrop of our sermon series. We have looked at Mark 8: 1-9 where Jesus took seven baskets of bread and fish and feed 4,000 people. We Looked at Mark 8:11-21, where Jesus did not answer them, but he got into a ship and moved on, Then we looked at Mark 8:22-26 where Jesus healed a blind man by touching him two times. Now in this homiletical diamond in the ruff we come to Mark 8:27-30.

What I have failed to mention is that this text is synoptic. This question that has caused much debate theologically is housed in Matthew 16:13-16, Luke 9:18-20, and in Mark 8: 27-30. There are some textual differences in the different text when you do a textual comparison. Mark says Jesus asked the question while they were on the way to Caesarea Philippi. While Matthew and Luke leave those words out.

Matthew describes Jesus as the Son of Man while Mark and Luke just says, "who do men say that I am?" Matthew is concerned with Jesus' divinity and humanity. Matthew is also the only one that adds Matthew 16:18. And I say also unto thee, That thou art Peter, and upon this rock I will build my church; and the gates of hell shall not prevail against it. The church has withstood all the fiery darts of the devil, all the winds of adversity, and all that the world has tried to do to the church because Jesus declared the gates of hell shall not prevail against it.

We are told that Jesus and His disciples are in the *"cities of*

Caesarea Philippi". This was a predominately Gentile area located some 25 miles north of Bethsaida where Jesus had just healed the blind man, **Mark 8:22-26**. It is here that a spring issues forth from Mount Hermon that forms one of the tributaries that becomes the Jordan River.

This was a beautiful area that was steeped in pagan religion. In ancient time, the city had been called "*Balinas*", because it had been a center of Baal worship. Baal was the Phoenician god of fertility and nature.

Later, the name was changed to "*Panias*", because the Greeks believed that their god Pan was born in a cave in the hills above the city, at the foot of Mount Hermon. Pan was a half-goat, half-man god who was believed to be the guardian of flocks and nature. In fact, the modern name of this ancient city is "*Banias*", which is a form of "*Panias*".

Caesarea Philippi also contained a gleaming marble temple, built by Herod Philip, to honor Caesar, the Roman Emperor, who was considered to be a god. The citizens of this city were required to enter this temple, at least once per year, place a pinch of incense on a burning altar and proclaim, "*Caesar is Lord!*"

It was here, in this city devoted to the worship of idols and manmade gods that Jesus chose as the place to make a fuller revelation of Himself to His disciples. It was also here that Simon Peter saw for the first time that Jesus Christ was truly the Son of God.

The Lord's first question is this: "*Whom do men say that I am?*" Jesus knew what the people were saying about Him. He was not paranoid, nor was He seeking the praise of men. Jesus intended to use to opinions of the people, concerning His identity, to cause the disciples to think about their own opinions of just Who Jesus was. Every child of God ought to wrestle with this question. Who do you say Jesus is? Every born again believer ought to know who Jesus is for yourself. You can't live your whole life off of what someone else has said about Jesus.

Jesus has been good to you and you ought to proclaim that to the world....

Jesus is Mary's baby

Jesus is my bridge over trouble water

Jesus is both alpha and omega

Jesus is my storm calmer when life is falling apart

There is power in the name of Jesus

Devils tremble at the name of Jesus...........Has anybody tried Jesus lately...

When Jesus asks this question, His men tell Jesus want they have been hearing others say. They said some people say that you are, "***John the Baptist: but some say, Elias; and others, One of the prophets***." Let's take a moment to break their response down.

John the Baptist – Jesus certainly resembled John the Baptist in His preaching. Both men preached a message of repentance and righteousness. But, many people had seen Jesus and John together, so this response is kind of strange to me. Of course, Herod Antipas believed that Jesus was none other than John the Baptist raised from the dead, **Mark 6:14**. That is probably where that theory came from.

But John himself said

John 1:27 He it is, who coming after me is preferred before me, whose shoe's latchet I am not worthy to unloose. John knew that he did not come close to Jesus. Others believed that Jesus was Elijah raised from the dead. This makes a little more sense, because both Jesus and Elijah conducted a ministry that was marked by clear, convicting preaching and convincing miracles. Others believed that Jesus was "*One of the prophets*". This was a long list that included such luminaries as Moses, Daniel, Isaiah, Jeremiah, Hosea, and Elijah Mohammed others.

The Muslims believe that Jesus was just another prophet. But brother Muslim Jesus is more than just another prophet.

Jesus is King of Kings

Jesus is Lord of Lords

At the name of Jesus ever knee including Muslim knees will bow. Ever tongue will confess that Jesus is Lord including those that believe in Allah.

Like Moses, Jesus declared the Law of God. Like Isaiah, Jesus preached about sacrifice and holiness. Like Daniel, the message of Jesus was a prophetic message of a coming King and His kingdom.

Like Jeremiah, Jesus carried out a ministry marked by compassion and brokenness. He was, after all, "*a man of sorrows, and acquainted with grief*", **Isa. 53:3**. Like Hosea, Jesus loved the unlovable and was willing to redeem lost, wretched sinners.

That's what the people were saying, but other voices were also expressing their opinions about Jesus in that day.

The **Pharisees** and other religious elitists of the day said, *"...He hath a devil, and is mad; why hear ye him?"* **John 10:20**.

The **Scribes**, the men viewed as great teachers of the Law, said, "He hath Beelzebub, and by the prince of the devils casteth he out devils," Mark 3:22.

The **Sanhedrin**, the ruling body of the Jewish religion, said, "...He hath spoken blasphemy; what further need have we of witnesses? behold, now ye have heard his blasphemy. What think ye? They answered and said, He is guilty of death. Then did they spit in his face, and buffeted him; and others smote him with the palms of their hands, Saying, Prophesy unto us, thou Christ, Who is he that smote thee?" Matthew 26:65-68.

His Own family and friends said, *"He is beside himself,"* **Mark 3:21**.

That lets me know that sometimes even your own family will turn on you and not stand with you.....When you walking with the Lord you are going to be misunderstood.

You are going to have to shake some unwelcoming hands....

Some of the very ones who hug you will turn around try to stab you in the back. Some will even say that you not who God called you to be...But I read in the word that weeping may endure for a night but if you hold on joy gone come in the morning.......

Even as Jesus hung on the cross, giving His life a ransom for sin, the religious elite continued to express their evil opinion of

Him. "Likewise also the chief priests mocking said among themselves with the scribes, He saved others; himself he cannot save. Let Christ the King of Israel descend now from the cross, that we may see and believe. And they that were crucified with him reviled him," Mark 15:31-32.

We see that not everyone was wrong about who Jesus was.

Not every voice in that day was lifted against Jesus. Some people knew Who He was and proclaimed Him openly.

- John the Baptist got it right – **John 1:29-34**.
- John 1:15 John bare witness of him, and cried, saying, This was he of whom I spoke, He that cometh after me is preferred before me: for he was before me.
- The Angels got it right – **Luke 2:9-14.** Luke 2:10 And the angel said unto them, Fear not: for, behold, I bring you good tidings of great joy, which shall be to all people. Luke 2:11 For unto you is born this day in the city of David a Savior, which is Christ the Lord.
- Simeon got it right – Luke 2:25-35. Luke 2:29 Lord, now lettest thou thy servant depart
- in peace, according to thy word: Luke 2:30 For mine eyes have seen thy salvation,
- Anna got it right – Luke 2:36-38.
- The dying thief got it right – Luke 23:42. Luke 23:47 Now when the centurion saw what was done, he glorified God, saying, Certainly this was a righteous man.

- The Roman Centurion got it right – Mark 15:39. Mark 15:39 And when the centurion, which stood over against him, saw that he so cried out, and gave up the ghost, he said, Truly this man was the Son of God.
- The blind man got it right – John 9:38.
- Bartimaeus got it right – Mark 10:47.
- The crowds outside Jerusalem got it right – John 12:13.
- Even the demons got it right – Mark 5:7.

Mark 5:7 And cried with a loud voice, and said, What have I to do with thee, Jesus, thou Son of the most high God? I adjure thee by God, that thou torment me not.

We see next what they say about Jesus

That's what some of the people in that day were saying about Jesus. What are they saying about Him in our day? Just as it was in the days when Jesus walked this earth, there are a multitude of opinions about Who He was and is today.

- The Muslim says that Jesus was a prophet, but He was not crucified on a cross. He will return, but He is not God.
- The Hindu believes that Jesus is just one of millions of gods.
- The Jew believes that Jesus was a great prophet and teacher, but He is not God.

- The Mormon believes that Jesus was the first baby born to God in Heaven, when God, in a physical body, had sexual intercourse with Mary, His Own daughter. He is the spirit brother of Lucifer.

- The Jehovah's Witnesses believe that Jesus was once the Archangel Michael before He came to the earth. In their view Jesus is not God in the flesh.

- The atheist denies that Jesus ever existed at all.

- The agnostic doesn't know what to believe about Jesus.

- Society believes that Jesus was a great teacher; that He had some good ideas about loving your fellow man and being good to others, but they do not believe that He is the Savior, or that He is God in the flesh. Most people acknowledge His existence, but they refuse to bow to His authority or give Him the worship He deserves.

We have heard the theories and thoughts of men concerning Jesus. Before we leave this thought behind, we need to hear one more opinion. Listen to what God in Heaven has to say about this man called Jesus.

Now let's look at what the Bible says about Jesus

- When Jesus was baptized by John in Jordan, God the Father said, "This is my beloved Son, in whom I am well pleased," Matthew 3:17.

- When Jesus was transfigured, God the Father said, "This is my beloved Son, in whom I am well pleased; hear ye him,"

Matthew 17:5.

- If God the Father says that Jesus is His Son that is good

Part II Jesus Asks A Personal Question V. 29-30

After hearing His disciples tell Him what others say, Jesus asks them for their opinion. He has heard public opinion, now He wants to hear their personal opinion.

This is the moment of truth! Everything Jesus has taught them and shown them has been leading up to this moment in time. Every miracle was leading to this one moment in time. Every word of truth Jesus spoke was being His men to this great spiritual crossroad. Their response to this question would let Jesus know how effective His personal ministry to these men had been.

Jesus simply asks, *"But, Whom say ye that I am?"* It is a simple question, but it is filled with eternal implications. A correct answer to that question takes one to Heaven; an incorrect answer to that question takes one to Hell.

Peter, as was his custom, spoke for the whole group. Peter said, *"Thou art the Christ!"* He got it right!

In Matthew's account of these events, Matthew quotes Peter as saying, *"Thou art the Christ, the Son of the living God,"* **Matt. 16:16**.

There in Caesarea Philippi, against that backdrop of paganism and false religion, Peter saw in a humble, homeless carpenter from Nazareth the very essence of God Himself. Peter looked at Jesus and saw the Messiah, which is what the word "***Christ***" means.

It is a title and not a name. It literally means "***The anointed One***." Peter also saw Jesus as the "***Son of God***." What a statement of faith! It is made even more amazing by the fact that up to this point, only God and demons have recognized the identity of the Lord Jesus.

Of course, Peter did not come to the knowledge on his own. **Matthew 16:17** says, "***And Jesus answered and said unto him, Blessed art thou, Simon Barjona: for flesh and blood hath not revealed it unto thee, but my Father which is in heaven***".

There are somethings that only God can reveal to you. You have to walk close to God and God will walk close to you.....

The Lord's identity was revealed to Peter by God Himself. This is true in every genuine conversion, **John 6:44**. No one is saved by the persuasive opinions of men. People are saved when their spiritual eyes are opened by the Lord. He gives them the faith to believe unto salvation, **Eph. 2:8-9**.

Peter's declaration lets us know that Peter was a saved man. He knew Who Jesus was and he openly confessed Him. Peter was saved, but not all of the disciples were.

In that group that day stood a man by the name of Judas Iscariot. He probably believed what Peter said in his head, but he never acted on that belief in faith. Judas died lost, and was, by Jesus 'Own testimony, a "***devil***", **John 6:70**.

This just serves to remind us that your opinion about Who Jesus is, is a very personal thing.

No one can speak for you.

No one can believe for you.

In the end, it does not matter what anyone else has to say about Who Jesus is; it all comes down to Who you believe He is.

Your answer to the Lord's question is absolutely vital to your salvation.

How you answer that question will determine where you spend eternity. Jesus is still asking, "But whom say ye that I am?" What is your answer?

Maybe you are like the atheist and you don't believe in Jesus or God. Friend, you are sinning against the light! You are willfully closing your eyes to the facts that are all around you, Psa. 19:1-4.

Maybe you are like the agnostic; you just don't believe that anyone can be sure about such things. Friend, you are also sinning against the light. Look at the changed lives all around you and understand that people do not possess the power to make such radical change; it is a God thing, 2 Cor. 5:17.

Maybe you hold to some of the false beliefs of the cults and other religions regarding Jesus. Friend, here is the truth: "For God so loved the world, that he gave his only begotten Son, that whosoever believeth in him should not perish, but have everlasting life." John 3:16. "Jesus saith unto him, I am the way, the truth, and the life: no man cometh unto the Father, but by me," John 14:6. "I said therefore unto you, that ye shall die in your sins: for if ye believe not that I am he, ye shall die in your sins," John 8:24.

Maybe you think Jesus was just a great teacher or a great

leader of men. You believe He existed, but not that He is the only Savior of men. Listen to what C.S. Lewis said about people who believe like you. "A man who was merely a man and said the sort of things Jesus said would not be a great moral teacher. He would either be a lunatic - on the level with a man who says he is a poached egg - or he would be the devil of hell. You must take your choice. Either this was, and is, the Son of God, or else a madman or something worse. You can shut Him up for a fool or you can fall at His feet and call Him Lord and God. But let us not come with any patronizing nonsense about His being a great human teacher. He has not left that open to us."

Peter believed Jesus was God, Lord and Savior, and he was saved. All of the disciples believed Jesus was God. Lord and Savior and they were all saved. Millions have believed the same thing about Him over the last 2,000 years and they have all been saved.

The issue today is, what do you believe about Jesus? You will make a judgment concerning Him today. You will either receive Him or reject Him, but you will make a judgment concerning Jesus Christ today.

If Jesus were to look you in the eye today and say "Who do you say that I am"; what would your answer be? Could you say, "Jesus, I believe You are the Son of God. I believe You are the Savior of the world. I believe You are my Savior." Or would you have to say, "In spite of all the evidence, I reject You Jesus. In spite of what the Bible says; in spite of what God says; in spite of what millions of believers say; I will not receive you into my heart and life."

How you answer the Lord's question will determine where you will spend eternity. Where will it be? Will you go to Heaven? Or, will you go to Hell?

What is your final answer? Who is Jesus to you? Hear Who the Bible says He is.

- **A**-Adam, Advocate, Anointed, Apostle, Author, Amen, Alpha, Ancient of Days.
- **B**-The Beginning, the Begotten, Beloved, Branch, Bread, Bridegroom, Bright and Morning Star, Bishop of our souls, Brightness of the Father's glory.
- **C**-Captain of our Salvation, Consolation, Chief Cornerstone, Counselor, Covenant, Chosen of God, Christ.
- **D**-The Daysman, Deliverer, Dayspring, Daystar, Door, Desire of all nations.
- **E**-The Elect, Ensign, Emmanuel, Everlasting Father.
- **F**-Finisher of our faith, Friend, Forerunner, First Fruits, Faithful Witness, Fountain of life issuing from the cave of death.
- **G**-God, Gift of God, Governor, Guide, Glorious Lord.
- **H**-Help, Hope, Husband, Horn of Salvation, Hearer, Head of the Church, Heir of all things, High Priest, Hell's dread, Heaven's wonder - the Holy One.

- **I**-I Am, Inheritance, Image of God's Person, Immortal and Invisible.

- **J**-Judah, Just, Judge, Jesus.

- **K**-King of Israel, King of Kings, King of Glory, King Everlasting.

- **L**-The Life, the Light, Love, Lily, Lion, Lamb, Lawgiver, Living Stone, the Lord of glory.

- **M**-Messenger, Mediator, Master, Messiah, Mighty God, Mercy's Paradox.

- **N**-The Nazarene.

- **O**-Offspring of David, Omega, Only Begotten of God, Offering and Offerer.

- **P**-Priest, Passover, Potentate, Prophet, Propitiation, Prince of Life, Prince of Peace, Physician.

- **Q**-Conquer King

- **R**-Righteousness, Rabbi, Ransom, Rest, Root of Jesse, Root of David, Refiner, Refuge, Resurrection, Rose of Sharon, Ruler, Rock of Ages, Regenerate Breath.

- **S**-Stone, Shepherd, Son of God, Son of Man, Shield, Servant, Seed of the Woman, Surety, Sufferer, Savior, Sinless Sacrifice, the Same Yesterday, Today and Forever.

- **T** -Teacher, Truth, Tabernacle, Testator, Treasure, Tree of Life.

- **W**-Witness, Word, Way, Wisdom of God, Wonderful.

WHAT TO DO WHEN GOD'S PLAN DOESN'T MAKE SENSE

Mark 8:33 But when he had turned about and looked on his disciples, he rebuked Peter, saying, Get thee behind me, Satan: for thou savourest not the things that be of God, but the things that be of men. I have enjoyed walking through Mark the 8th chapter out of this one chapter we looked at verses 1-8 when Jesus feed the 4,000 and we told you that God will supply. We also looked at verses 11-13 and told you to keep moving, because ever situation does not deserve a response. Then we traveled to verses 22-26 when Jesus had to touch the man twice before he was healed, and we called it a second touch. Next we looked at verses 27-30 and asked you do you know him for yourself. And last Sunday we went to the end of the pericope and looked at verses 34-38 and asked you about your journeys end.

This Sunday we have been divinely arrested and captured by the Holy spirt to look at verses 31-33. Walk back with me to Mark's Gospel for the last time in this eight chapter. It was the movie a Few Good Men. In that movie for those of you who have seen it can remember this scene. Lt. Daniel Kaffee (Tom Cruise) is a military lawyer defending two U.S. Marines charged with killing a fellow Marine at the Guantanamo Bay Naval Base in Cuba. Although Kaffee is known for seeking plea bargains, a fellow lawyer, Lt. Cdr. JoAnne Galloway (Demi Moore), convinces him that the accused marines were most likely carrying out an order from a commanding officer. Kaffee takes a risk by calling Col. Nathan R. Jessep (Jack Nicholson) to the stand in an effort to uncover the conspiracy. Jack Nicholson then says these unforgettable line he says you can't handle the truth.

As we come to vs. 31 we are returning to a conversation that's already in progress. In vs. 29 Peter has just made a great declaration – confessing his belief that Jesus is the Christ – the Messiah, the redeemer of Israel. Matthew 16:18 And I say also unto thee, That thou art Peter, and upon this rock I will build my church; and the gates of hell shall not prevail against it. It's a significant moment in the Gospel of Mark, but it's immediately followed by a seemingly odd command from Jesus. Jesus, knowing that the disciples don't yet fully understand the ministry of the Messiah, commands His disciples not to tell anyone what they believe about Him.

Then when we come to verse 31 we notice that Jesus **spoke plainly -** While Jesus had often spoken in parables or through signs and miracles, Mark tells us in vs. 31 that in this case He speaks plainly. Jesus is not speaking in hyperbole or in metaphorical language. He's speaking openly and clearly. He is telling His disciples what it means for Him to be the Messiah. He must suffer, die and rise.

Mark 8:31 Then He began to teach them that the Son of Man must suffer many things and be rejected by the elders, the chief priests, and the scribes, be killed, and rise after three days. In other words Jesus tells his disciples the truth and apparently they can't handle the truth. They are not yet ready for open and honest conversation about what Jesus is getting ready to face. When Jesus finally tells them what God's plan is for his life it does not make sense to them. How do you handle God's plan for life when it seems like they don't make any sense? What do you do when God's direction for your future leaves you with more questions than answers?

When Jesus spoke of the suffering and death of the Messiah his disciples could not believe what they were hearing. All their lives they had connected the Messiah with a power-figure who would save God's people from their oppressors. Therefore the idea of a suffering Messiah just did not make any sense. This idea of a Jesus who would submit himself to author of another and be beaten even to the point of death does not make sense. As a matter of fact Jesus says it like this "Then He began to teach them that the Son of Man must suffer many things" He looked down through time and saw the thorns that would be placed on his head and pressed in skull. He peeped over in time and saw the cat of 9 tails that would rip flesh from his bones. He even saw the day that he would be blind folded and the soldiers mocking him and saying prophecy who it is that hit you.

He looked around the corner of space and eternity and saw him carrying his own cross up skull mountain and said the son of man is going to suffer many things. I like to pause and pull over and tell you that you can handle the **many things** that you go through in this life because Jesus was able to handle the **many**

things he went through. As a matter of fact he went through them so you and I would not have to go through them. Not only did Jesus say he would suffer many things he said who would be the cause of the suffering. Notice verse 31 c clause "and be rejected by the elders, the chief priests, and the scribes." The first group were "the elders." These were religious leaders in the community. They were wealthy, powerful, and influential. The second group were "the leading priests." They supervised the temple and the sacrificial system.

The third group were "the teachers of religious law." These were the approved interpreters of the Old Testament, and they were mostly Pharisees. They were the theologians and lawyers of Judaism who were experts in Israel's religious laws. Jesus knew who the bullies where. Jesus knew who the hate, torture and misfortune would come from. Nothing catches God off guard. If Jesus was able to handle his bullies you can handle your bullies as well. What you are dealing with does not catch God off guard. Cancer doesn't catch God off guard. Diabetes doesn't catch God off guard. High Blood pressure doesn't catch God off guard. Bullies and haters don't catch God off guard…. Stand still and let God fight your battle….If you fight all your battles then you want have no need for God to intervene…..Some stuff is best left up to God to handle.

Notice he told his disciples that he would be killed, and rise after three days. He told them the **beginning** be killed, He them the **middle** be buried, and he them the **end** after three days he was going to rise form the dead. We serve a risen savior. We serve a savior that rose from the grave with all power in his hands......What a marvelous God we serve.....Who wouldn't serve a God like this. We see in the text that Jesus spoke plainly and then we see that Peter rebuked him privately. Mark 8:32 He was openly talking about this. So Peter took Him aside and began to rebuke Him. The Message Bible says it like this: **32** But Peter grabbed him in protest.

In others words Peter like so many of us can't handle the truth, or we can say that Peter is having a hard time with what was just said because God's plan is not making sense to him. **A bold rebuke** – Most likely as the spokesman for the rest of the disciples, Peter goes to Jesus and rebukes Him for suggesting that He will suffer and die (Matthew 16:22). The word translated as *rebuke* is the same word used earlier in Mark when Jesus is ordering demons to listen and obey. Peter is bold and assertive in his stand against Christ. He rebukes Jesus without any idea that what Jesus is describing is the plan of salvation that was established before the foundation of the world.

Jesus you just feed 4, 000 people why you talking about death. Jesus you just healed a blind man with the spite from your mouth, why you talking about death. Jesus looks at the mega church that is following you and attention you are getting from all these people. No one has ever seen numbers like this before. Jesus you are at the height of your ministry you should be talking about progression, not doom and death. It's easy to shake our heads at Peter's rebuke of Jesus, but we are all prone to similar foolishness. We are quick to position ourselves against God when we don't understand what He's doing.

You have been at the company for years and still have not got the promotion or position and you have asked God several times God what are you doing. You have been asked to be a flower girl at everybody wedding and have even caught the bokeh and your day still has not come and you are asking God what are you doing. As a matter of fact you told God my child bearing years are almost over what are you doing? You exercised every day, ate right, and drank only water but you still got sick and now you are asking God what are you doing....**God this that I am going through just don't make sense**......So Peter makes a bold rebuke of Jesus.....

Then Jesus makes a public rebuke of Peter not in private but public. How do you handle your private conversation with Jesus now that it's front page news and everyone now knows what you just did. Notice how the message Bible puts it "Peter, get out of my way! Satan, get lost! You have no idea how God works." Jesus responds Mark 8:33 But turning around and looking at His disciples, He rebuked Peter and said, "Get behind Me, Satan, because you're not thinking about God's concerns, but man's!" **A public rebuke** – While Peter had pulled Jesus to the side, Mark makes it clear that Jesus rebukes Peter in the presence of all of the disciples. This probably indicates that Peter is the spokesman and they all deserve the rebuke He receives. They were thinking what he was bold enough to say. They were just as guilt for thinking the same way as him...

If you know something is not right don't follow the crowd. If you know someone is being bullied say something. You just might be the one to save that person's life. **Get behind me, Satan -** Jesus uses strong language to draw attention to the seriousness of the offense. Not only are the disciples questioning Jesus, they are, in a sense, suggesting that He abandon the course that would lead to salvation. This is the kind of thing that the devil desires and the same tactic He used when He tempted Jesus in the wilderness. **The devils desire is to get you off course.** The devils desire is to get you to abandon God's plan for life that He told you to do.

When you do what God tells you it going to make some people mad, it's going to cause you to be unpopular, it's going to cause you to have to stand alone and be misunderstood but if you know God said it then stand on it. If you know you are doing the will of God, God will see you through. Isn't it interesting how the devil tries to persuade us through the words of a well-meaning friend to play it safe in our lives. Sometimes it's those that are close to us that tries to get us away from the plan of God. Sometimes, an opportunity for Christian service, or an opportunity to stand up for justice and peace comes our way. In our hearts we are absolutely convinced that this is from God, and that he is calling us to obey His will. We know that it will cost us a lot in terms of "losing" some of the comforts that we have grown used to. However, we are at peace with our decision, knowing that it is God's will. As we share our decision with family and friends, they raise one red flag after another. Has this ever happened to you?

Look at somebody and if God said it I am standing on it. You see, the Devil is very clever. Without our knowledge he uses the people who are closest to us to break our spirits and our obedience to God. Peter was that special friend, who just a little while earlier had received a revelation from God when he confessed, "You are Christ, the Son of the living God." Peter's good intentions and his dedication to his Master kept him from seeing God's divine plan of salvation for humankind.

Jesus saw through the well-meaning words of his disciple. He caught the devil in the act, and called him on the carpet. Jesus was fully focused on God's agenda, not his own. My testimony is "I'm staying focused on God's agenda not mine, not yours, and not there's but God's". Did you hear what I said "I'm staying focused on God's agenda not mine, not yours, and not there's but God's". If God don't tell me to reveal my plan of action until God say so, take it up with God. Jesus is not calling Peter the devil. He is pointing out the truth that Peter is speaking the words of Satan. He is telling Peter that He is being used as a tool by the devil. Jesus is not sending Peter away; He is commanding Satan to leave.

Help me preach tell Satan he got to go

He got get his hands off the church

He got leave our families alone

He got leave my wife alone

He got to leave my husband alone

He got to leave my children alone

He got to leave my community alone…

He got to go…

I don't care where he go but he got to get out of here…

Then Jesus tells them that their real problem is that they are looking at His ministry through the eyes of men and not through the eyes of God. They were looking for power, glory and position. Jesus knew those things were in God's plan, but only after He had suffered for sin on the cross. God's plan involved the death of the Messiah and anyone who opposed that plan was doing the work of Satan! This is the same man who just called Jesus "The Christ", verse 29. One minute Peter is declaring deep spiritual truth, the next moment he is doing the work of the devil! There are a couple of thoughts that we need to consider here.

We are often just like Peter. We look at everything around us through human eyes. We only see how things affect us. We only care about our comfort, our needs and our wishes. The will of God is a million miles away from our thinking. That needs to change, Eph. 6:6.

Ephesians 6:6 Not with eyeservice, as menpleasers; but as the servants of Christ, doing the will of God from the heart;

Men care about the material; God cares about the eternal.

Men care about prosperity; God cares about holiness.

Men care about power; God cares about purity!

Men care about flesh; God cares about the future!

Often we fail to see that there is a very thin line between doing the Lord's work and doing the devil's work. It is vitally important that every thought be taken captive and brought to Jesus, 2 Cor. 10:5; and that every action is screened through the filter of the Word and will of God, 1 Thes. 5:22.

One final thought:

When a fellow believer has a "Peter Moment", when they fail the Lord in a big way, the rest of us should help them get back where they ought to be with the Lord, Gal. 6:1-2. We all have our "Peter Moments", but that does not mean that our usefulness and effectiveness are at an end. It simply means that we need to pick up the pieces and move on for the glory of God! In other words Jesus was telling Peter that I am going to run on and see what the end gone be.

Jesus was telling Peter serving the Lord will Pay off after a while. Peter only knew the part of the story and life that he could see, but what Peter failed to realize is that Jesus knew the end of the story. You don't know how it's going to turn out but God knows just how things are going to work out in your life. Since Jesus knows the end of my story I need to trust Him when things don't make sense.

This is just a chapter of my life, it's not the end of my story.

Keep reading it gets better.

Keep holding on it gets better.

Better days are coming.

Joy is coming.

WHAT WILL YOU FIND AT LIFE'S END

Jesus would have been a public relations manager's nightmare! Every time He began to attract a large following, Jesus would up the ante. He would tell them how high the cost of following Him would be and the crowds would vanish. Jesus did this so that people would know the truth. He wanted them to know that it would not be cheap or easy to be His disciples. By the way, it is a serious thing to make a profession of faith or to join a church! In this verse, Jesus shares a pattern for true discipleship.

Let me remind you that not everyone who claims to be a Christian can truly be called a disciple of Jesus. The church and those that say they love the Lord have given up on the race too easily. We have more empty pews and less commitment now more than ever before. Those who would be His disciples, His followers have four requirements that they must meet in this life. Let me share them with you today. Jesus says whosoever-whosoever does not have a limit on it, it is an all-encompassing word. Whosoever includes all those who want to be saved. Whosoever is not gender specific. Whosoever does not have race, nationality, or origin attached to it. Whosoever will come after me. You are in included in the whosoever crowd.

"Come After Me" When Jesus said these words, His men surely remembered when He first called them to follow Him. Some two and a half years ago, they had left everything to follow Jesus. They had left family, friends, occupations, and everything else in their lives to go with Jesus.

If you have not left anything to follow Jesus is your walk with Jesus a genuine walk? If you can hold onto your Jesus and your same way of life, Have you really followed Jesus? To the rest of the crowd that day, this was a call to the new birth. It was a call to make a personal commitment to Jesus Christ. It was a call for them to turn their backs on everything else to go after Jesus. You can fool some of the people some of the time but you can't fool all of the people all of time. Whatever you do for Jesus let it be real.

> Let your serving be real
>
> Let your singing be real
>
> Let your praying be real
>
> Let your witness be real.

Being born again, getting saved, or whatever you want to call it, is far more than praying a prayer at an altar. A lot of people come to an altar, pray a prayer and profess to know Jesus Christ on Sunday but act like they don't know him on Monday. True salvation is about a radical commitment to leave the old life behind to follow Jesus into a new and very different life. Being born again is about being made a "new creation", 2 Corinthians 5:17.

2 Corinthians 5:17 Therefore if any man be in Christ, he is a new creature: old things are passed away; behold, all things are become new. All things, your speech becomes new, your walk becomes new, your habits become new, your level of faith becomes new. What use to shake you don't bother you anymore because you are a new creature in Christ Jesus. That person that

ran upon you the other day better be glad you not the person you use to be because the outcome would have been different, the conversation would have been different but thanks be to God you been changed. You see, you can pray the Sinner's Prayer all day and not get saved.

You walk the Roman Road, take a Journey through John, or go through any other method that people say brings salvation. The fact is, you only get saved when God convicts you of your sins and draws you to Himself, **John 6:44**. John 6:44 No man can come to me, except the Father which hath sent me draw him: and I will raise him up at the last day. Aren't you glad that one day Jesus drew you to himself. Jesus took time to change your life. When He draws you and you respond by faith, salvation takes place, **Ephesians 2:8-9.** (Some people here are in a dangerous place – **Gen. 6:3.**)

True salvation, however is not some form of "*easy believing*" that leaves you unchanged. True salvation, when it happens in your life, will make such a radical change in your life that you will begin to act like a different person. Your desires and habits will change. Your interests and commitments will change. Sisters He can't treat you any kind of way and get away with because you been changed. Brothers she can't sweet talk you and you give in because you been changed. Who can say I know I been changed because the angels in heaven done signed my name.

When you come to Jesus Christ and are truly saved, you will want to follow Him. Where Jesus is, is where you will desire to be

"Come After Me."

To the lost person it is a call to be saved. Are you saved?

"Come After Me."

To the saved person it is a call to radical commitment. Are you totally, truly and radically following Jesus today?

"Come After Me."

To the confused it brings clarity of direction. Not only does this text gives birth to direction. It highlights denial of desire. Slide

"Deny Himself" This phrase literally means, *"to completely disown, to utterly separate oneself from someone."* It is the same word used to describe Peter's denial of Jesus outside the high priests home, **Matt. 26:34**! Matthew 26:34 Jesus said unto him, Verily I say unto thee, That this night, before the cock crow, thou shalt deny me thrice. Denying self is not the same thing as self-denial. Some people will practice self-denial by withholding certain things from themselves, like some high church people do during Lent. That is not what Jesus is talking about.

Denying self is far more intense than that. Denying self implies that I stop listening to my own voice. I stop leaning on my own power. I stop trying to fulfill my own will and wishes. When I truly deny myself, I have no will but His will. I have no plans but His plans. I have no wants but what He wants for me. When I deny myself, I give up all my rights and I relinquish all control of my life to the Lord Jesus Christ. I live out **1 Cor. 6:19-20**, *"What? know ye not that your body is the temple of the Holy Ghost which* *is in you, which ye have of God, and ye are not your own? For ye are bought with a price: therefore glorify God in your body, and in your spirit, which are God's.*" You die to yourself because you belong to someone else, the Lord.

That is a concept that is foreign in our day! Most religions and most popular ministries are focused on catering to self. They want people to feel good about themselves. They want to build up people's self-esteem. They want mankind to rejoice in his achievements and in his abilities. They want to present a gospel that is cheap and cost you nothing. Jesus, on the other hand, wants mankind to know that without Him, they are nothing and can do nothing, **John 15:5**. Jesus is calling those who claim Him as their Savior to make a total commitment to His Lordship in their lives. He wants absolute control in every area of our lives. He calls on us to disown ourselves and give Him the reigns of our lives. This phrase suggests a "*once for all action*". We are to deny ourselves and to forget about us. Notice this verse presents us with **direction**, **denial of desire**, and it gives us a **duty to follow**.

"Take Up His Cross" This phrase had much meaning for the people in Jesus 'day. Historians estimate that over 30,000 people were crucified by the Romans during Jesus 'lifetime. Thus, every person who heard Jesus say these words knew what He was saying to them.

In that day, a cross was not a piece of jewelry or a decoration on a church building. A cross was an instrument of shame, humiliation, suffering, torture and death. When a man took up his cross, he was **beginning a death march**. His life was taken on new meaning. Take your cross meant For God I live and For God I'll die. When a man took up his cross, he carried the instrument of his own death on his own shoulders. When he reached his destination, he was laid down on the cross he had carried; he was nailed to it; he suffered on it and he die on it. When Jesus called these people to take up their cross, they knew exactly what He was talking about! Sadly, that message has become clouded in our day. The message has gotten lost in translation in this **cross-less generation.** A generation where people want to have their cake and eat it too. In this Burger King generation they want religion and Jesus there way.

Some people think that the burdens of life are a cross they must bear. Some people say that a lost, abusive spouse, a wayward child or a crazy boss is their cross. Some people think that an illness or a physical handicap is their cross. The trials and hardships you face in this life are not your cross! When Jesus tells His disciples to take up their cross and follow Him, He is calling us to **die to ourselves**. He is calling us to commit to a lifestyle of living death, **Gal. 2:20**.

Galatians 2:20 I am crucified with Christ: nevertheless I live; yet not I, but Christ liveth in me: and the life which I now live in the flesh I live by the faith of the Son of God, who loved me, and gave himself for me. He is calling us to willingly bear the *shame*, the *reproach*, the *humiliation*, the *suffering*, the *hatred*, the alienation and even the *death* that may come to those who are associated with Him. We take up our cross when we choose the narrow way over the way of the world, regardless of the cost. We take up our cross when we live out biblical ethics in our personal lives and in our business relationships, regardless of the cost.

We take up our cross when we are willing to suffer any attack for Jesus 'sake. You take up your cross endure the shame when folk call you everything but a child of God and anything but something good-have you been there. You take up your cross when it seems like you are the only one trying to live right, do right, and be right......have you been there. Not many people are truly carrying their cross today. Many are quick to compromise when it makes their way just a little easier. When they have to stand up against those that don't want to move forward in the church the lay down there cross for friendship.

When it's time to take a stand for progress they digress in the name of those that have not been to Red Oak, stop coming to Red Oak, and ain't coming back to Red Oak.

Businessmen will lie to keep their customers. Christians will lie to save face. Church folks will compromise with the world to avoid being singled out and humiliated for being a believer. To take up your cross means that you are willing to identify yourself with Jesus Christ, His death and His word, regardless of what it costs you personally, publicly or financially! That's not a side of Christianity you hear about very often! It isn't popular to talk about sacrifice, death and suffering, but that is what Christianity is all about! There are no cheap seats, but there is a high price to pay for being a genuine disciple of the Lord Jesus Christ. Just ask Paul – **2 Corinthians 11:23-28; 12:7-11**.

Does Jesus have any real ride or die saints in the house? Does Jesus have any For God I live and for God I'll die saints in the house? Who can say I am totally committed to Christ? By the way, this phrase also suggests a *"once for all"* action. I am to take up my cross and **never** lay it down until I reach the place of my death. This text has given birth to direction, denial of desire, duty to do, and now it gives birth to discipleship.

*"**Follow Me**"* – The true disciple of Jesus turns his back on his self and his old life. The true disciple of Jesus takes up his cross and is willing to lay down everything for the glory of God. The true disciple of Jesus takes his place behind the Lord and he follows Jesus wherever He leads. The true disciple walks in total obedience and submission to the Lord Jesus Christ!

True disciples tithe they don't tip God. True disciples are committed they don't comprise there values and morales. This phrase suggests *"**ongoing**"* action. Jesus is calling His people to be constant followers. Some people follow on Sunday, but take a different path on Monday. Some people follow the Lord when they need help, but take another path when things get better. Some people follow depends on which crowd they with-when they with the church friends they love the lord, when they with the **blues** crowd anything goes.

That is not what the Lord is looking for! Jesus is calling for His people to make a radical commitment to follow Him all the time, all the way to the end of their lives. I am trying to teach you today that there are no cheap grace in this thing called Christianity. It costs something to be a follower of the Lord Jesus Christ. And, only those willing to follow Him all the way have the goods, **Matt. 7:21-23**. Can we honestly say that we are totally committed to Jesus when other things in life come before Him? Can we honestly say that we are following Him when we do as we please when we please? Can you honestly say that you are bearing your cross when you can't even be faithful to the church attendance, Bible study, Sunday School, and tithing? Isn't it about time that God's children examined the priorities so that Jesus Christ and His will came first?

II. V. 35-37 Jesus Shares a Paradox

These three verses are designed to teach us that the spiritual side of our lives is far more important than the material side. That is not the way most people think. Most people live their entire lives trying to take care of the physical and material needs they have in life, while they give little attention to the spiritual side of life. Jesus wants us to know that only the spiritual side of life really matters in the end.

The Way To Save Your Life Is To Lose It – **v. 35** – This verse is a paradox. A paradox is a statement that seems contradictory but is still true. Jesus says that if you believe that having your own way, living life on your own terms and being your own lord is more important than surrendering to His Lordship, you will lose your life. However, if you will yield your life to Him, giving up total control over all you have and are to Him, you will actually save it. From a human perspective this makes no sense, but from heaven's viewpoint, nothing else makes sense.

You have a choice.

You can live your life as you see fit.

You can refuse to come to Jesus Christ for salvation. You can call all the shots.

You can be your own boss.

You can do as you please, living your life on your own terms, but in the end, you will lose your life.

When you reach the end of your way, you will find that there is nothing but an eternity in Hell waiting for you. On the other hand, you can commit your life to Jesus. You can deny your own will, give up all your rights, surrender to His Lordship and follow Him faithfully. At the end of that way, His way, you will find that the door of Heaven will be opened to you. So, in the economy of God, "*Losers are Keepers*." Those who lose their lives by giving them up for Jesus are winners in the end. While those who live for this life alone, lose everything in the end. What kind of ending do you anticipate? There are no cheap seats!

In **verses 36**, Jesus asks a powerful question. Think about it for just a moment. Mark 8:36 For what shall it profit a man, if he shall gain the whole world, and lose his own soul? Imagine that you possessed the whole world and all the riches in it. Imagine that you could do anything you wanted to do, be anything you wanted to be, or go anywhere you wanted to go. Imagine that you were the absolute ruler of all things material. Sounds like a dream come true doesn't it?

Now, imagine at the end of that experience of having, being and doing as you please that you die. Now, imagine that after death you found yourself in Hell forever. Would those few years, or even decades, of pleasure be worth an eternity in a law of fire. Jesus told a story about a man who experienced such a fate, **Luke 16:19-31**. That man lived his life in the lap of luxury and then he died and went to Hell. When he arrived there, all the money, all the pleasure and all the power he had enjoyed in this life were useless to him in Hell. He had lost his soul, thus, he had lost everything.

Let's be realistic. Most people in this room will never know what it is like to possess riches, power and the ability to do as you please. So, imagine that you live your life, doing all the things that you want to do, and when you reach the end of your life you die. You have worked hard all your life. You have done without, endured hardship and suffered, but you have lived life on your terms.

Then you die and still; go to Hell. Where is the profit in that? What have you gained? You have gained nothing, but you have lost everything! That's why you need to come to Jesus and you need to do it today.

Jesus asks another powerful question in **verse 37**. *What is the worth of your soul?* Before you answer, let me remind you that your soul is the only part of you that will live forever. Your body will die and be buried, but you soul will live on in either Heaven above or in Hell beneath. So, what is your soul worth.

Are you willing to trade your eternal soul for some alcohol or drugs?

Are you willing to trade your soul for some sexual relationship?

Are you willing to trade your soul for the right to do as you please and live life on your own terms?

Are you willing to spend eternity in Hell for a few years of being your own god?

If you are lost, that is exactly what you are doing! You are trading the most valuable possession you have for the trinkets of this world. You have bought into the lie of the devil and you are going to lose all you have and all you are in a place called the underworld. Listen to this preacher: It's not too late to change the road you are on. Come to Jesus today and trade this world in for a permanent, eternal relationship with Him. Trade Hell for Heaven today! Slide

(Ill. In about 1,000 AD the tomb of Charlemagne, the King of the Franks, was opened. The great king had been dead for about 180 years by then. When they opened his tomb, they found great treasure, but they also encountered an amazing site. They saw the skeleton of Charlemagne sitting on throne, with a crown still sitting on the skull. In the bony hands of that skeleton was a copy of the Gospels. A bony finger was pointing to this text, *"For what shall it profit a man, if he shall gain the whole world, and lose his own soul? Or what shall a man give in exchange for his soul?"*

Charlemagne was a great king, but in the end, none of that mattered. When it came time for him to die, he left his robes, his riches and his royalty behind and he went out into eternity to meet his God. When you and I reach the end of our earthly journey, nothing we have achieved or accumulated in this life will matter. All that will matter in that hour is our relationship with the Lord Jesus Christ. All that will matter is that we willingly lost our lives to His will so that He might live through us.

What will you find at your journey's end?

When I come to the end of my journey I want people to say I was faithful to the church.

When I come to end of my journey I want people to say I was a good husband to my wife.

When I come down to the end of my journey here I want people to say I was a good father to my son Joshua.

When I come done to end of my journey I want people to say I when I preached I preached sound messages.

But what I most want to hear servant well done. Well done thou good and faithful servant you been faithful over a few things come on up and I will make you ruler over many. Who else want hear well done in order to hear well done- you have to do well.

Reverend Dr. Jeffery A. Gladney

ABOUT THE AUTHOR

Reverend Dr. Jeffery Gladney

Dr. Gladney has truly been blessed to matriculate through some of God's best colleges and universities in the world. He was an honor graduate of Rust College in Holly Springs, Mississippi where he received his Bachelor of Science degree in Early Childhood Education. He studied Evangelism, Ecumenism, and Missiology (World Religion) at the Interdenominational Theological Center; Morehouse School of Religion in Atlanta, Georgia where he again graduated with honors.

He also studied at United Theological Seminary in Dayton, Ohio where he earned his Doctor of Ministry degree. The topic of his dissertation was "Reconnecting the Local Church and Community through Multilateral Ecumenical Unity: The Church Speaking as One Voice with One Purpose."

Dr. Gladney is married to the former Valeria Moore of Clarksdale, Mississippi. She has been by his side and continues to work with him achieving all that God has for the both of them as a strong Christian couple in the Lord. They have one son Joshua A. Gladney.

He believes in the Sankofa method which means "return and get it" - we learn from the past which ensures a strong future.

Dr. Gladney has served in the following positions: *Dean, Congress General Progressive Baptist State Convention Of Ms. Inc, Second Vice-President, General Progressive Baptist State Convention of Mississippi, Inc. Second Vice Moderator Springhill District Baptist Association, Teacher, National Baptist Convention of America International, Inc. Teacher, Spring Hill District Baptist Association, Tupelo, MS, Teacher, Home Mission Board/Congress General Progressive Baptist State Convention of*

Mississippi, Inc. Teacher/Coordinator, ITC Certificate In Theology Program, Instructor Northeast Community College Old Testament, Director of Mississippi Baptist Seminary and Bible College Tupelo Extension.

BIBLIOGRAPHY

Brindle, Wayne A, and et, al.. *The King James Study Bible.* Nashville, Tennessee: Thomas Nelson Publishers , 1988

Cordell Steve. *The Church In Many Houses Reaching Your Community Through   Cell Based Ministry,* Abingdon Press Nashville, *2005*

Conn Harvie. *God So Loves The City,* World Vision International, Monrovia, Ca, 1994

Dawn Marva, Peterson Eugene. *The Unnecessary Pastor, Rediscovering The Call,* Regent College Publishing Vancouver, Grand Rapids Michigan, 2000

Holmes T. Urban III. *Spirituality For Ministry,* Morehouse Publishing, Harrisburg, Pennsylvania, 1930

Linthicum Robert C. *Empowering The Poor Community Organizing Among the City's Rag, Tag and Bobtail,* World Vision International, Monrovia, California, 1991

Linthicum Robert C. *Transforming Power,* World Vision International, Monrovia, California, 2003

McCalep O. George. *Faithful Over A Few Things,* Orman Press, Lithonia Georgia, 1996

McNeal Reggie, *The Present Future Six Tough Questions For The Church,* Jossey-Bass A. Wiley Imprint, San Francisco, Ca. 2003

Sisemore T. John, Church Growth Through the Sunday School, Boardman Press, Nashville, Tennessee 1983

Smith Edward L. Process and The Black Experience *A Series In Postmodern Study,* The Research Press-Marion Frank Smith, Riverdale, Georgia, 2000

Stewart Caryle III. *African American Church Growth 12 Principles for Prophetic Ministry,* Abingdon Press, Nashville, Tennessee, 1994

Wilkins Rob, Lewis Robert. *The Church Of Irresistible Influence,* Zondervan, Grand Rapids, Michigan, 2001

www.ingramcontent.com/pod-product-compliance
Lightning Source LLC
Chambersburg PA
CBHW051220120626
46547CB00013B/1442